CHARLES LAMB ON SHAKESPEARE

George Frederick Cooke as Richard III. Portrait (1811) by Thomas Sully.

CHARLES LAMB
ON SHAKESPEARE

Edited by Joan Coldwell

820788

BARNES & NOBLE
BOOKS
10 East 53d St., New York 10022
(a division of Harper & Row Publishers, Inc.)

Contents

Illustrations

Notes on Sources

The extracts from Lamb's published works are reprinted from *The Works of Charles and Mary Lamb*, edited by E. V. Lucas, 7 vols. (London: Methuen, 1903-1905), hereafter referred to as *Works*. Passages from the correspondence up to 1809 are from *The Letters of Charles and Mary Anne Lamb*, edited by Edwin W. Marrs, Jr. 2 vols. (Cornell University Press, 1975-1976), hereinafter referred to as *Letters*. Quotations from Lamb's later correspondence are from *The Letters of Charles and Mary Lamb*, edited by E. V. Lucas, 3 vols. (London: J. M. Dent and Methuen, 1935).

J. P. Collier's notes are in *Coleridge's Shakespearean Criticism*, edited by T. M. Raysor, 2 vols. (London: J. M. Dent, 1930). Henry Crabb Robinson's *Diary, Reminiscences and Correspondence* is edited by Thomas Sadler, 2 vols. (London, 1869).

Quotations from Shakespeare in the editorial matter are from William Shakespeare, *The Complete Works*, edited by Peter Alexander (London: Collins, 1951).

Acknowledgements

I am most grateful to The Pennsylvania Academy of Fine Arts for permission to reproduce Sully's portrait of G. F. Cooke, the Theatre Collection of the Metropolitan Toronto Central Library for permission to reproduce Mortimer's portrait of Bensley and Powell and the engraving of Mrs Siddons as Lady Macbeth, and to the Osborne Collection of the Metropolitan Toronto Central Library for the engravings from Lamb's *Tales from Shakespear*.

Introduction

Long before he found his own creative form in the familiar essay, Charles Lamb had developed a solid, if limited, reputation as a Shakespearean critic. Many of the illustrious friends who gathered for his regular evenings of cards, food and good talk testified to his perceptiveness. Coleridge for example spoke of Lamb's 'exquisite criticisms on Shakespeare'[1] and Hazlitt thought him a sounder authority than either Johnson or Schlegel 'on any subject in which poetry and feeling are concerned'.[2] Another friend wrote: 'Of that greatest of all poets he has said such things as I imagine Shakespeare himself would have liked to hear.'[3]

Barry Cornwall's choice of compliment here suggests two significant points about Lamb's criticism. 'He has said such things': Lamb's influence as a Shakespearian began in talk and, in spite of his bad stammer, it was through memorable phrases, astute shafts of wit and pithy summaries that his reputation developed. He had neither the desire nor the capacity for sustained critical argument, claiming that he was temperamentally unsuited to a methodical approach to literature. Perhaps this was a reaction to the routine of his East India House clerkship, work which certainly left him little time for preparing any substantial commentary. Most of his published criticism came out first as periodical pieces and there is only one essay, apart from theatre reviews, devoted entirely to Shakespeare. The rest is fragmentary, a passage here or there in general essays or letters, and always the tone of the conversationalist is maintained. Indeed, one virtue of Lamb's criticism is precisely the virtue of fine talk: by flashes of perception, neatly worded and founded on complete familiarity with the subject, the reader is challenged to articulate his own responses and test his own judgment. But the fact that Lamb's comments on Shakespeare are scattered throughout his work has made them relatively inaccessible and his reputation as a critic has inevitably suffered.

The type of praise Cornwall thought suitable for Lamb's criticism is also revealing. One feature of the Romantic absorption in Shakespeare was a feeling of personal involvement with him, the belief in an initiate's intuitive grasp of his meaning. Lamb was by

11

no means alone in his sense of almost mystical identification with Shakespeare. Keats provides perhaps the most familiar examples of this kind of empathic response and a passage in one of his theatre reviews admirably illustrates the coterie spirit: 'The acting of Kean is Shakesperian; – he will fully understand what we mean.'[4] When Wordsworth attempted to shift the god Shakespeare from his pinnacle, Lamb rose to the challenge with a response that, in spite of its humour, is typically possessive and personal: 'after one has been reading Shaksp. twenty of the best years of one's life, to have a fellow start up, and prate about some unknown quality, which Shakspere possess'd in a degree inferior to Milton *and somebody else*! ! '[5] While such passion and enthusiasm have little validity as a rational base for criticism, it is nevertheless true that, in the work of men who are in addition informed, well-read and intelligent, they give rise to an invaluable extra dimension of insight.

Lamb claimed to have been reading Shakespeare since the age of six and it is by no means out of the ordinary for a precocious boy, particularly one with access to a fine private library,[6] to start so young. In his adult years Lamb read Shakespeare closely and often, keeping extract books and making careful notes of unusual words. He frequently read the plays aloud to his sister, 'winter evenings, the world shut out',[7] and by these means came to have the texts at his fingertips, so that quotations and allusions cropped up naturally and often unconsciously in his own writing. When Lamb first tried his hand at a play, it was almost inevitable that he should attempt to imitate the master: 'I go upon the model of Shakspere in my play, and endeavour after a colloquial ease and spirit something like him.'[8] With his friend Jem White he collaborated on a pseudo-forgery, *The Falstaff Letters*, a clever imitation of Shakespeare's style which, however, gained no reputation in spite of Lamb's firm belief in its quality.

Although theatregoing was frowned on at Christ's Hospital School, Lamb had an early start in this also, having seen his first play at Drury Lane when he was six. He saw his first Shakespearean production, *Twelfth Night*, at the age of sixteen and the details of it stayed in his memory for years. The theatrical world was in fact part of his everyday life; at one time he lived directly opposite the Drury Lane Theatre and was easily visited there by the many actors who formed part of his intimate circle. He missed very few of the productions and saw some of the century's greatest performers, among them Kemble, Kean and Mrs Siddons. It is all the more surprising, then, that his most famous critical essay should begin with a vehement attack on the cult of the actor and take as its theme the rejection of stage performances of Shakespeare's plays.

Like Coleridge, Hazlitt and De Quincey, Lamb held that Shakespearean drama is best appreciated in the reader's own imagination and can only suffer diminution on stage. He knew that his views were shaped in part by the far from ideal conditions of the early nineteenth century theatre, where Shakespeare's own texts were seldom if ever used, where costumes and settings either lacked design or strove too hard for 'realism' and where oratorical method emphasized the artificiality of such conventions as the soliloquy and the aside. But Lamb could not apparently visualize any theatrical style in which the plays could be performed to his ideal standards. This was not so of all drama; Lamb does not argue against theatre in general but he distinguishes between types of play suited to stage performance. The distinction is based on characterization. Some playwrights draw their characters from life, as in the comedy of manners, and real human beings fittingly personate them on stage. But Shakespeare's characters, in the Romantic view, are products of the poet's imagination, not imitations of 'those cheap and every-day characters which surrounded him, as they surround us.' Therefore, as characters of imagination, they will most nearly be approached through the imagination of a reader. They are abstract, and to give them visible form is, in Lamb's view, to bring down 'a fine vision to the standard of flesh and blood.' To Lamb an actor can only be an obstruction between Shakespeare's concept of the character and his own perception of it; everything about stage performance distracts, costume, gesture, style of speech, even the actor's own personality ('we speak of Lady Macbeth, while we are really thinking of Mrs S.[iddons].')[9] It is the visual aspect that is most disturbing because it draws attention away from the intellectual and inner to the outward and superficial parts of a character.

The imaginative understanding of character is Lamb's chief contribution to criticism and he was one of the first to explore the many-sidedness of Shakespeare's characters. His most original and perceptive study is of Richard III, a plea for the playing of a human Richard instead of a melodramatic monster. One can trace the gradual development of Lamb's view from the time he saw Cooke's performance of the role in 1801 through successive rethinkings to a simple summary in the essay on the tragedies ten years later. His analysis of Malvolio, in whose fall he sees a 'kind of tragic interest', is more controversial but again it illustrates a method of looking at character in depth, for human comprehensiveness rather than as stage caricature. In this Lamb may be said to have foreshadowed the concerns of modern psychological criticism.

Lamb knew himself to have been a pioneer in studies of Shakespeare's fellow dramatists. In his autobiographical sketch he wrote: 'He also was the first to draw the Public attention to the old English Dramatists in a work called "Specimens of English Dramatic Writers who lived about the time of Shakespeare".'[10] Lamb's interest in this drama was fostered by his love of old books. He owned, among many rare volumes, a folio edition of Beaumont and Fletcher, already virtually unattainable by 1804, and he copied extracts from this and others into his letters so that friends might share his delight. This was the chief motive behind his decision to publish extracts from the collection of old plays in the British Museum, but he was also concerned, as he wrote in the Preface, to show 'how much of Shakspeare shines in the great men his contemporaries, and how far in his divine mind and manners he surpassed them and all mankind.' Lamb's notes to the plays touch on comparative themes, such as the contrast between Richard II and Marlowe's Edward II, to be developed by twentieth century critics.

In yet another area Lamb, together with his sister, did pioneering work and in this case it has not been bettered. *The Tales from Shakespear* are clear and forceful narrative condensations of the plays, which do not talk down to their young audience but show, in their skilful paraphrasing, a firm mastery of Shakespeare's complex language and thoughts. Lamb was responsible for the tragedies and in his selection of details and emphases one can observe the influence of his general critical approach. The Macbeth story provides a good illustration. Although Lamb intended to make only such alterations as were necessary to provide 'easy reading for very young children', he here seems rather to introduce changes to fit his own interpretation of the tragedy.

We know from a conversation recorded by H. C. Robinson that Lamb considered Lady Macbeth a 'hardened being', 'one of Shakespeare's worst characters'. Thus in the tale she is forcefully

14

categorized as a 'bad, ambitious woman'. Lamb goes further than Shakespeare in making her actively evil. For instance, his Lady Macbeth plans from the beginning to murder Duncan herself. This is possibly a justifiable reading of her:

> What cannot you and I perform upon
> Th' unguarded Duncan.

When the resemblance to her father shakes her courage she returns to Macbeth 'and with the valour of her tongue she so chastized his sluggish resolutions, that he once more summoned up courage to the bloody business.'

To increase the sense of Lady Macbeth's villainy, Lamb alters the episodes so that Macbeth does nothing evil of his own planning. He does not kill the grooms, nor does he plan the murder of Banquo without his wife's connivance. 'Be innocent of the knowledge, dearest chuck', he says in the play, but in Lamb's story 'they determined to put to death both Banquo and his son.' The sleep-walking scene is omitted, lest sympathy for the queen develop, and Lamb simply says that the two 'had their sleeps afflicted with terrible dreams.'

Though A. H. Thompson may seem to exaggerate when he calls the *Tales* 'one of the most conspicuous landmarks in the history of the romantic movement', he is right in asserting that it was the 'first book which, appealing to a general audience and to a rising generation, made Shakespeare a familiar and popular author.'[11] It is fortunate that the work of popularizing Shakespeare was done upon so solid a foundation of knowledge and poetic sensitivity as Lamb possessed. He himself would surely have been more delighted by that wide communication of his pleasure in Shakespeare than by the accolades of more scholarly critics.

Such critical acclaim has not of course been lacking. For almost a century after his death Lamb had an enthusiastic following; Pater and Swinburne both lavished extravagant praises on his Shakespearean criticism and A. C. Bradley, about to carry Lamb's method of character study to its limits, referred to him as 'the best critic of the nineteenth century'.[12] Although Lamb's reputation as critic is now overshadowed by that of Coleridge and of Hazlitt, the voice of praise is still sometimes heard, as in J. Dover Wilson's claim that Lamb's discussion of Richard III cannot be bettered.[13]

Lamb himself, with even his Elia essays receiving inadequate attention in his lifetime, could not have seen his place in the history of Shakespeare studies. And yet he had a very clear awareness of his own critical strength, as the following anecdote illustrates. Lamb was once at a dinner with De Quincey, whose essay 'On the knocking at the gate in *Macbeth*' is probably more widely known than any of Lamb's criticism. Pointing to De Quincey, Lamb said: 'Do you see that little man? Well, though he is so little, he has written a thing about Macbeth better than anything I could write; – no – not better than anything I could write, but I could not write anything better'.[14] It is for such qualities of honesty, clearsightedness and a confidence based on knowledge and experience that Lamb's criticism is still to be valued.

I Richard the Third

Most of Lamb's comment on 'Richard III' stems from his reaction to G. F. Cooke's playing of the title role. Cooke (1756–1811) first appeared at the Covent Garden Theatre in the 1800–1801 season, making his name with a Richard very different from the one presented during the previous two decades by J. P. Kemble. Lamb saw Cooke's performance during the first season and wrote vigorously about his initial response to it in a letter of 26 June, 1801. Six months afterwards he contributed a belated review of the performance to the 'Morning Post' and, after ten years, referred to it again in his essay 'On the tragedies of Shakspeare'.

The text of 'Richard III' as then played was not Shakespeare's but the 'improved' version created by Colley Cibber in 1700. Lamb violently objected to the omissions, interpolations and alterations, but Cibber's text was generally popular and it held the stage until 1845. Cibber's 'Richard III' is reprinted in 'Five Restoration Adaptations of Shakespeare', ed. Christopher Spencer (University of Illinois, 1965).

Cooke in Richard the Third is a perfect caricature. He gives you the *monster* Richard, but not the *man* Richard. Shakespear's bloody character impresses you with awe and deep admiration of his witty parts, his consummate hypocrisy, and indefatigable prosecution of purpose. You despise, detest, and loathe the cunning, vulgar, low and fierce Richard, which Cooke substitutes in his place. He gives you no other idea, than of a vulgar villain, rejoycing in his being able to over reach, and not possessing that joy in *silent* consciousness, but betraying it, like a *poor* villain in sneers and distortions of the face, like a droll at a country fair: [1] not to add that cunning so self-betraying and manner so vulgar could never have deceived the politic Buckingham, nor the soft Lady Anne: *both*, bred in courts, would have turned with disgust from such a fellow. – Not but Cooke has *powers*; but not of discrimination. His manner is strong, coarse & vigorous, and well adapted to some characters. – But the lofty imagery and high sentiments and high passions of *Poetry* come black & prose-smoked from his prose Lips. . . .

I am possessed with an Admiration of the genuine Richard, his genius, and his mounting spirit, which no consideration of his cruelties can depress. Shakespear has not made Richard so black a Monster, as is supposed. Wherever he is monstrous, it was to conform to vulgar opinion. But he is generally a Man. Read his most exquisite address to the Widowed Queen to court her daughter for him, the topics of maternal feeling, of a deep knowledge of the heart, are such as no monster could have supplied. Richard must have *felt*, before he could feign so well; tho' ambition choked the good seed. I think it the most finished piece of Eloquence in the world; of *persuasive* Oratory, far above Demosthenes, Burke,[2] or any man. – Far exceeding the courtship of Lady Anne. – *Her* relenting is barely natural after all; the more perhaps S's merit to make *impossible* appear *probable*, but the *Queen's consent* . . . is *probable;* . . . This observation applies to many other parts. All the inconsistency is, that Shakespeare's better Genius was forced to struggle against the prejudices, which made a monster of Richard. He set out to paint a *monster*, but his human sympathies produced a *Man* —

Are you not tired with this *ingenious* criticism? I am. . . .

Richard itself is wholly metamorphosed in the wretched *Acting play* of that name, which you will see: altered by *Cibber*. —

From a letter to Robert Lloyd, 26 June, 1801.

Some few of us remember to have *seen*, and all of us have heard our fathers tell of Quin, and Garrick, and Barry,[3] and some faint traditional notices are left us of their manner in particular scenes, and their stile of delivering certain emphatic sentences. Hence our curiosity is excited, when a *new Hamlet* or a *new Richard* makes his appearance, in the first place, to inquire, how he acted in the *Closet scene*, in the *Tent scene*; how he looked, and how he started, when the *Ghost* came on, and how he cried

Off with his head. So much for Buckingham.[4]

We do not reprehend this minute spirit of comparison. On the contrary, we consider it as a delightful artifice, by which we connect the recreations of the past with those of the present generation, what pleased our fathers with what pleases us. We love to witness the obstinate attachments, the unconquerable prejudices (as they seem to us), of the old men, our seniors, the whimsical gratification they appear to derive from the very refusal to be gratified; to hear them talk of the good *old* actors, whose race is for ever extinct.

With these impressions, we attended the first appearance of Mr Cooke, in the character of *Richard the Third*, last winter. We thought that he 'bustled' through the scenes with at least as much spirit and effect as any of his predecessors whom we remember in the part, and was not deficient in the delivery of any of those rememberable speeches and exclamations, which old prescription hath set up as *criteria* of comparison. Now that the grace of freshness is worn off, and Mr Cooke is no longer a novitiate candidate for public favour, we propose to enter into the question – whether that popular actor is right or wrong in his conception of the great outlines of the character; those strong essential differences which separate *Richard* from all the other creations of Shakespeare. We say *of Shakespeare*; for though the Play, which passes for *his* upon the *Stage*, materially differs from *that* which *he* wrote under the same title, being in fact little better than a compilation or a cento of passages extracted from other of his Plays, and applied with gross violations of propriety (as we are ready at any time to point out), besides some miserable additions, which *he* never could have written; all together producing an inevitable inconsistency of character, sufficient to puzzle and confound the *best Actor; yet*, in this chaos and perplexity, we are of opinion, that it becomes an Actor to shew his taste, by adhering, as much as possible, to the spirit and intention of the original Author, and to consult his *safety* in *steering* by the *Light*, which Shakespeare holds out to him, as by a great *Leading Star*. Upon these principles, we presume to censure Mr Cooke, while we are ready to acknowledge, that this Actor presents us with a very original and very forcible portrait (if not of the *man Richard*, whom Shakespeare drew, yet) of the *monster Richard*, as he exists in the *popular idea*, in *his own exaggerated* and *witty self-abuse*, in the overstrained representations of the parties who were *sufferers* by his *ambition*; and, above all, in the impertinent and wretched *scenes*, so absurdly foisted in by some, who have thought themselves capable of adding to what *Shakespeare wrote*.

But of Mr Cooke's *Richard*:

1st. *His predominant and masterly simulation*
       He has a tongue can wheedle with the DEVIL.[5]

J. P. Kemble.

It has been the policy of that antient and grey simulator, in all ages, to hide his *horns* and *claws*. The *Richard* of Mr Cooke perpetually obtrudes *his*. We see the effect of his deceit uniformly *successful*, but we do not comprehend *how* it *succeeds*. We can put ourselves, by a very common fiction, into the place of the individuals upon whom it acts, and say, that, in the like case, we should not have been alike credulous. The hypocrisy is too glaring and visible. It resembles more the shallow cunning of a mind which is its own dupe, than the profound and practised art of so powerful an intellect as *Richard's*. It is too obstreperous and loud, breaking out into *triumphs* and *plaudits* at its own success, like an unexercised *noviciate* in *tricks*. It has none of the silent confidence, and steady self-command of the *experienced politician*; it possesses none of that *fine address*, which was necessary to have betrayed the heart of *Lady Anne*, or even to have imposed upon the duller wits of the *Lord Mayor* and *Citizens*.

2dly. *His habitual jocularity*, the effect of buoyant spirits, and an elastic mind, rejoicing in its own powers, and in the success of its machinations. This quality of unstrained mirth accompanies *Richard*, and is a prime feature in his character. It never leaves him in plots, in stratagems, and in the midst of his bloody devices, it is perpetually driving him upon wit, and jests and personal satire, fanciful allusions, and quaint felicities of phrase. It is one of the chief artifices by which the consummate master of dramatic effect has contrived to soften the horrors of the scene, and to make us contemplate a bloody and vicious character with delight. No where, in any of his plays, is to be found so much of sprightly colloquial dialogue, and soliloquies of genuine humour, as in *Richard*. This character of unlaboured mirth Mr Cooke seems entirely to pass over, and substitutes in its stead the coarse, taunting humour, and clumsy merriment, of a low-minded assassin.

3dly. *His personal deformity*. – When the *Richard* of Mr Cooke makes allusions to his own *form*, they seem accompanied with *unmixed distaste* and *pain*, like some obtrusive and *haunting* idea – But surely the *Richard* of Shakespeare mingles in these allusions a perpetual reference to his own powers and capacities, by which he is enabled to surmount these petty objections; and the joy of a defect *conquered*, or *turned* into an advantage, is one cause of these very allusions, and of the satisfaction, with which his mind recurs to them. These allusions themselves are made in an ironical and

21

good humoured spirit of exaggeration – the most bitter of them are to be found in his self-congratulating soliloquy spoken in the very moment and crisis of joyful exultation on the success of his unheard of courtship. – No *partial excellence* can satisfy for this absence of a *just general conception* – otherwise we are inclined to admit, that, in the delivery of *single sentences*, in a *new* and often *felicitous* light thrown upon *old* and *hitherto misconstrued* passages, no actor that we have seen has gone beyond Mr Cooke. He is always *alive* to the scene before him; and by *fire* and *novelty* of his manner, he seems likely to infuse some *warm blood* into the *frozen declamatory stile*, into which our theatres have for some time past been degenerating.

'G. F. Cooke in "Richard the Third" ',
Morning Post, 8 January, 1802.

These old play-wrights[6] invested their bad characters with notions of good, which could by no possibility have co-existed with their actions. Without a soul of goodness in himself, how could Shakspeare's Richard the Third have lit upon those sweet phrases and inducements by which he attempts to win over the dowager queen to let him wed her daughter? It is not Nature's nature, but Imagination's substituted nature, which does almost as well in a fiction.

Note to 'Extracts from the Garrick Plays',
Home's Table Book, 1827.

> And since I cannot, I will prove a *villain*,
> And hate the idle pleasures of these days.
> *Soliloquy in Richard III*[7]

The performers, whom I have seen in this part, seem to mistake the import of the word which I have marked with italics. Richard does not mean, that because he is by shape and temper unfitted for a *courtier*, he is therefore determined to prove, in our sense of the word, a *wicked man*. The word in Shakspeare's time had not passed entirely into the modern sense; it was in its passage certainly, and indifferently used as such; the beauty of a world of words in that age was in their being less definite than they are now, fixed, and petrified. *Villain* is here undoubtedly used for a *churl*, or *clown*, opposed to a *courtier*; and the incipient deterioration of the meaning gave the use of it in this place great spirit and beauty.[8] A *wicked man* does not necessarily hate *courtly pleasures*; a *clown* is naturally opposed to them. The mistake of this meaning has, I think, led the players into that hard literal conception with which they deliver this passage, quite foreign, in my understanding, to the bold gay-faced irony of the soliloquy. Richard, upon the stage, looks round, as if he were literally apprehensive of some dog snapping at him; and announces his determination of procuring a looking-glass, and employing a tailor, as if he were prepared to put both in practice before he should get home – I apprehend 'a world of figures here'.[9]

'Scraps of Criticism', *London Magazine*, December, 1822.

Lamb maintained that the most impressive dream he had ever read was Clarence's, in 'Richard III',[10] which was not now allowed to form part of the acted play. There was another famous dream in Shakespeare, that of Antigonus in the 'Winter's Tale',[11] and all illustrated the line in Spenser's 'Fairy Queen', Book IV.c.5:

'The things which day most minds at night do most appear';[12] the truth of which every body's experience proved and therefore every body at once acknowledged.

J. P. Collier's notes of a conversation.

II The Tragedies

Lamb first gained a footing as a periodical essayist in Leigh Hunt's paper 'The Reflector'. This short-lived publication ran for only four numbers, 1810-1811, but it carried fourteen pieces by Lamb, most of them later reprinted in his 'Works' (1818). Lamb's longest critical essays, 'On the Genius of Hogarth' and 'On the Tragedies of Shakspeare', appeared in Nos. III and IV respectively.

When Lamb contributed the Elia essays to the 'London Magazine', between 1820 and 1825, he wrote always with Shakespeare at the back of his mind. Although no Elia essay is devoted solely to Shakespeare's plays, quotations and allusions abound and there are several short critical comments interspersed with the more general matter.

Taking a turn the other day in the Abbey,[1] I was struck with the affected attitude of a figure, which I do not remember to have seen before, and which upon examination proved to be a whole-length of the celebrated Mr Garrick. Though I would not go so far with some good catholics abroad as to shut players altogether out of consecrated ground, yet I own I was not a little scandalized at the introduction of theatrical airs and gestures into a place set apart to remind us of the saddest realities. Going nearer, I found inscribed under this harlequin figure the following lines:–

> To paint fair Nature, by divine command,
> Her magic pencil in his glowing hand,
> A Shakspeare rose: then to expand his fame
> Wide o'er this breathing world, a Garrick came.
> Though sunk in death the forms the Poet drew,
> The Actor's genius bade them breathe anew;
> Though, like the bard himself, in night they lay,
> Immortal Garrick call'd them back to day:
> And till ETERNITY with power sublime,
> Shall mark the mortal hour of hoary TIME,
> SHAKSPEARE and GARRICK like twin stars shall
> shine,
> And earth irradiate with a beam divine.[2]

It would be an insult to my readers' understandings to attempt any thing like a criticism on this farrago of false thoughts and nonsense. But the reflection it led me into was a kind of wonder, how, from the days of the actor here celebrated to our own, it should have been the fashion to compliment every performer in his turn, that has had the luck to please the town in any of the great characters of Shakspeare, with the notion of possessing a *mind congenial with the poet's*: how people should come thus unaccountably to confound the power of originating poetical images and conceptions with the faculty of being able to read or recite the same when put into words;* or what connection that absolute mastery over the heart and soul of man, which a great dramatic poet possesses, has with those low tricks upon the eye and ear, which a player by observing a few general effects, which some common passion, as grief, anger, &c. usually has upon the gestures and exterior, can so easily compass. To know the internal workings and movements of a great mind, of an Othello or a Hamlet for instance, the *when* and the *why* and the *how far* they should be moved; to what pitch a passion is becoming; to give the reins and to pull in the curb exactly at the moment when the drawing in or the slackening is most graceful; seems to demand a reach of intellect of a vastly different extent from that which is employed upon the bare imitation of the signs of these passions in the countenance or gesture, which signs are usually observed to be most lively and emphatic in the weaker sort of minds, and which signs can after all but indicate some passion, as I said before, anger, or grief, generally; but of the motives and grounds of the passion, wherein it differs from the same passion in low and vulgar natures, of these the actor can give no more idea by his face or gesture than the eye (without a metaphor) can speak, or the muscles utter intelligible sounds. But such is the instantaneous nature of the impressions which we take in at the eye and ear at a playhouse, compared with the slow apprehension oftentimes of the under-

*It is observable that we fall into this confusion only in *dramatic* recitations. We never dream that the gentleman who reads Lucretius in public with great applause, is therefore a great poet and philosopher; nor do we find that Tom Davies, the bookseller,[3] who is recorded to have recited the Paradise Lost better than any man in England in his day (though I cannot help thinking there must be some mistake in this tradition) was therefore, by his intimate friends, set upon a level with Milton. [Lamb's note]

J.Rhamberg del.ᵗ   Delattre sc.

Mᵣˢ SIDDONS in LADY MACBETH.

"Yet here's a Spot

Printed for John Bell, British Library London; Augᵗ 26.1784.

standing in reading, that we are apt not only to sink the play-writer in the consideration which we pay to the actor, but even to identify in our minds in a perverse manner, the actor with the character which he represents. It is difficult for a frequent playgoer to disembarrass the idea of Hamlet from the person and voice of Mr K.[4] We speak of Lady Macbeth, while we are in reality thinking of Mrs S.[5] Nor is this confusion incidental alone to unlettered persons, who, not possessing the advantage of reading, are necessarily dependent upon the stageplayer for all the pleasure which they can receive from the drama, and to whom the very idea of *what an author is* cannot be made comprehensible without some pain and perplexity of mind: the error is one from which persons otherwise not meanly lettered, find it almost impossible to extricate themselves.

Never let me be so ungrateful as to forget the very high degree of satisfaction which I received some years back from seeing for the first time a tragedy of Shakspeare performed, in which these two great performers sustained the principal parts.[6] It seemed to embody and realize conceptions which had hitherto assumed no distinct shape. But dearly do we pay all our life after for this juvenile pleasure, this sense of distinctness. When the novelty is past, we find to our cost that instead of realizing an idea, we have only materialized and brought down a fine vision to the standard of flesh and blood. We have let go a dream, in quest of an unattainable substance.

How cruelly this operates upon the mind, to have its free conceptions thus crampt and pressed down to the measure of a strait-lacing actuality, may be judged from that delightful sensation of freshness, with which we turn to those plays of Shakspeare which have escaped being performed, and to those passages in the acting plays of the same writer which have happily been left out in performance. How far the very custom of hearing anything *spouted*, withers and blows upon a fine passage, may be seen in those speeches from Henry the Fifth, &c. which are current in the mouths of school-boys from their being to be found in *Enfield Speakers*,[7] and such kind of books. I confess myself utterly unable to appreciate that celebrated soliloquy in Hamlet, beginning 'To be or not to be,' or to tell whether it be good, bad or indifferent, it has been so handled and pawed about by declamatory boys and men, and torn so inhumanly from its living place and principle of

27

continuity in the play, till it is become to me a perfect dead member.

It may seem a paradox, but I cannot help being of opinion that the plays of Shakspeare are less calculated for performance on a stage, than those of almost any other dramatist whatever. Their distinguished excellence is a reason that they should be so. There is so much in them, which comes not under the province of acting, with which eye, and tone, and gesture, have nothing to do.

The glory of the scenic art is to personate passion, and the turns of passion; and the more coarse and palpable the passion is, the more hold upon the eyes and ears of the spectators the performer obviously possesses. For this reason, scolding scenes, scenes where two persons talk themselves into a fit of fury, and then in a surprising manner talk themselves out of it again, have always been the most popular upon our stage. And the reason is plain, because the spectators are here most palpably appealed to, they are the proper judges in this war of words, they are the legitimate ring that should be formed round such 'intellectual prize-fighters.' Talking is the direct object of the imitation here. But in all the best dramas, and in Shakspeare above all, how obvious it is, that the form of *speaking*, whether it be in soliloquy or dialogue, is only a medium, and often a highly artificial one, for putting the reader or spectator into possession of that knowledge of the inner structure and workings of mind in a character, which he could otherwise never have arrived at *in that form of composition* by any gift short of intuition. We do here as we do with novels written in the *epistolary form*. How many improprieties, perfect solecisms in letter-writing, do we put up with in Clarissa[8] and other books, for the sake of the delight which that form upon the whole gives us.

But the practice of stage representation reduces every thing to a controversy of elocution. Every character, from the boisterous blasphemings of Bajazet[9] to the shrinking timidity of womanhood, must play the orator. The love-dialogues of Romeo and Juliet, those silver-sweet sounds of lovers' tongues by night; the more intimate and sacred sweetness of nuptial colloquy between an Othello or a Posthumus[10] with their married wives, all those delicacies which are so delightful in the reading, as when we read of those youthful dalliances in Paradise —

As beseem'd
Fair couple link'd in happy nuptial league,
Alone: [11]

by the inherent fault of stage representation, how are these things sullied and turned from their very nature by being exposed to a large assembly; when such speeches as Imogen addresses to her lord, come drawling out of the mouth of a hired actress, whose courtship, though nominally addressed to the personated Posthumus, is manifestly aimed at the spectators, who are to judge of her endearments and her returns of love.

The character of Hamlet is perhaps that by which, since the days of Betterton,[12] a succession of popular performers have had the greatest ambition to distinguish themselves. The length of the part may be one of their reasons. But for the character itself, we find it in a play, and therefore we judge it a fit subject of dramatic representation. The play itself abounds in maxims and reflexions beyond any other, and therefore we consider it as a proper vehicle for conveying moral instruction. But Hamlet himself – what does he suffer meanwhile by being dragged forth as a public schoolmaster, to give lectures to the crowd! Why, nine parts in ten of what Hamlet does, are transactions between himself and his moral sense, they are the effusions of his solitary musings, which he retires to holes and corners and the most sequestered parts of the palace to pour forth; or rather, they are the silent meditations with which his bosom is bursting, reduced to *words* for the sake of the reader, who must else remain ignorant of what is passing there. These profound sorrows, these light-and-noise-abhorring ruminations, which the tongue scarce dares utter to deaf walls and chambers, how can they be represented by a gesticulating actor, who comes and mouths them out before an audience, making four hundred people his confidants at once? I say not that it is the fault of the actor so to do; he must pronounce them *ore rotundo*,[13] he must accompany them with his eye, he must insinuate them into his auditory by some trick of eye, tone, or gesture, or he fails. *He must be thinking all the while of his appearance, because he knows that all the while the spectators are judging of it.* And this is the way to represent the shy, negligent, retiring Hamlet.

It is true that there is no other mode of conveying a vast quantity of thought and feeling to a great portion of the audience, who otherwise would never earn it for themselves by reading, and the intellectual acquisition gained this way may, for aught I know, be inestimable; but I am not arguing that Hamlet should not be acted, but how much Hamlet is made another thing by being acted. I have heard much of the wonders which Garrick performed in this part; but as I never saw him, I must have leave to doubt whether the representation of such a character came within the province of his art. Those who tell me of him, speak of his eye, of the magic of his eye, and of his commanding voice: physical properties, vastly desirable in an actor, and without which he can never insinuate meaning into an auditory, – but what have they to do with Hamlet? what have they to do with intellect? In fact, the things aimed at in theatrical representation, are to arrest the spectator's eye upon the form and the gesture, and so to gain a more favourable hearing to what is spoken: it is not what the character is, but how he looks; not what he says, but how he speaks it. I see no reason to think that if the play of Hamlet were written over again by some such writer as Banks or Lillo,[14] retaining the process of the story, but totally omitting all the poetry of it, all the divine features of Shakspeare, his stupendous intellect; and only taking care to give us enough of passionate dialogue, which Banks or Lillo were never at a loss to furnish; I see not how the effect could be much different upon an audience, nor how the actor has it in his power to represent Shakspeare to us differently from his representation of Banks or Lillo. Hamlet would still be a youthful accomplished prince, and must be gracefully personated; he might be puzzled in his mind, wavering in his conduct, seemingly-cruel to Ophelia, he might see a ghost, and start at it, and address it kindly when he found it to be his father; all this in the poorest and most homely language of the servilest creeper after nature that ever consulted the palate of an audience; without troubling Shakspeare for the matter: and I see not but there would be room for all the power which an actor has, to display itself. All the passions and changes of passion might remain: for those are much less difficult to write or act than is thought, it is a trick easy to be attained, it is but rising or falling a note or two in the voice, a whisper with a significant foreboding look to announce its approach, and so contagious the counterfeit appearance of any emotion is, that let the words be what they will, the look and tone shall carry it off and make it pass for deep skill in the passions.

30

It is common for people to talk of Shakspeare's plays being *so natural*; that every body can understand him. They are natural indeed, they are grounded deep in nature, so deep that the depth of them lies out of the reach of most of us. You shall hear the same persons say that George Barnwell is very natural, and Othello is very natural, that they are both very deep; and to them they are the same kind of thing. At the one they sit and shed tears, because a good sort of young man is tempted by a naughty woman to commit a *trifling peccadillo*, the murder of an uncle or so,* that is all, and so comes to an untimely end, which is *so moving*; and at the other, because a blackamoor in a fit of jealousy kills his innocent white wife: and the odds are that ninety-nine out of a hundred would willingly behold the same catastrophe happen to both the heroes, and have thought the rope more due to Othello than to Barnwell. For of the texture of Othello's mind, the inward con- struction marvellously laid open with all its strengths and weak- nesses, its heroic confidences and its human misgivings, its agonies of hate springing from the depths of love, they see no more than the spectators at a cheaper rate, who pay their pennies apiece to look through the man's telescope in Leicester-fields, see into the inward plot and topography of the moon. Some dim thing or other they see, they see an actor personating a passion, of grief, or anger, for instance, and they recognize it as a copy of the usual external effects of such passions; or at least as being true to *that symbol of the emotion which passes current at the theatre for it*, for it is often no more than that: but of the grounds of the passion, its correspondence to a great or heroic nature, which is the only worthy object of tragedy, – that common auditors know any thing

*If this note could hope to meet the eye of any of the Managers, I would entreat and beg of them, in the name of both the Galleries, that this insult upon the morality of the common people of London should cease to be eternally repeated in the holiday weeks. Why are the 'Prentices of this famous and well-governed city, instead of an amusement, to be treated over and over again with the nauseous sermon of George Barn- well?[15] Why *at the end of their vistoes* [vistas] are we to place the *gallows*? Were I an uncle, I should not much like a nephew of mine to have such an example placed before his eyes. It is really making uncle- murder too trivial to exhibit it as done upon such slight motives; – it is attributing too much to such characters as Millwood; – it is putting things into the heads of good young men, which they would never otherwise have dreamed of. Uncles that think any thing of their lives, should fairly peti- tion the Chamberlain against it. [Lamb's note] of this, or can have any such notions dinned into them by the mere strength of an actor's lungs, – that apprehensions foreign to them should be thus infused into them by storm, I can neither believe, nor understand how it can be possible.

We talk of Shakspeare's admirable observation of life, when we should feel, that not from a petty inquisition into those cheap and every-day characters which surrounded him, as they surround us, but from his own mind, which was, to borrow a phrase of Ben Jonson's, the very 'sphere of humanity,'[16] he fetched those images of virtue and of knowledge, of which every one of us recognizing a part, think we comprehend in our natures the whole; and oftentimes mistake the powers which he positively creates in us, for nothing more than indigenous faculties of our own minds, which only waited the application of corresponding virtues in him to return a full and clear echo of the same.

To return to Hamlet. – Among the distinguishing features of that wonderful character, one of the most interesting (yet painful) is that soreness of mind which makes him treat the intrusions of Polonius with harshness, and that asperity which he puts on in his interviews with Ophelia. These tokens of an unhinged mind (if they be not mixed in the latter case with a profound artifice of love, to alienate Ophelia by affected discourtesies, so to prepare her mind for the breaking off of that loving intercourse, which can no longer find a place amidst business so serious as that which he has to do) are parts of his character, which to reconcile with our admiration of Hamlet, the most patient consideration of his situation is no more than necessary; they are what we *forgive afterwards*, and explain by the whole of his character, but *at the time* they are harsh and unpleasant. Yet such is the actor's necessity of giving strong blows to the audience, that I have never seen a player in this character, who did not exaggerate and strain to the utmost these ambiguous features, – these temporary deformities in the character. They make him express a vulgar scorn at Polonius which utterly degrades his gentility, and which no explanation can render palatable; they make him shew contempt, and curl up the nose at Ophelia's father, – contempt in its very grossest and most hateful form; but they get applause by it: it is natural, people say; that is, the words are scornful, and the actor expresses scorn, and that they can judge of: but why so much scorn, and of that sort, they never think of asking.

So to Ophelia. – All the Hamlets that I have ever seen, rant and rave at her as if she had committed some great crime, and the audience are highly pleased, because the words of the part are satirical, and they are enforced by the strongest expression of satirical indignation of which the face and voice are capable. But then, whether Hamlet is likely to have put on such brutal appearances to a lady whom he loved so dearly, is never thought on. The truth is, that in all such deep affections as had subsisted between Hamlet and Ophelia, there is a stock of *supererogatory love*, (if I may venture to use the expression) which in any great grief of heart, especially where that which preys upon the mind cannot be communicated, confers a kind of indulgence upon the grieved party to express itself, even to its heart's dearest object, in the language of a temporary alienation; but it is not alienation, it is a distraction purely, and so it always makes itself to be felt by that object: it is not anger, but grief assuming the appearance of anger, – love awkwardly counterfeiting hate, as sweet countenances when they try to frown: but such sternness and fierce disgust as Hamlet is made to shew, is no counterfeit, but the real face of absolute aversion, – of irreconcileable alienation. It may be said he puts on the madman; but then he should only so far put on this counterfeit lunacy as his own real distraction will give him leave; that is, incompletely, imperfectly; not in that confirmed, practised way, like a master of his art, or, as Dame Quickly would say, 'like one of those harlotry players.'[17]

I mean no disrespect to any actor, but the sort of pleasure which Shakspeare's plays give in the acting seems to me not at all to differ from that which the audience receive from those of other writers; and, *they being in themselves essentially so different from all others*, I must conclude that there is something in the nature of acting which levels all distinctions. And in fact, who does not speak indifferently of the Gamester and of Macbeth as fine stage performances, and praise the Mrs Beverley in the same way as the Lady Macbeth of Mrs S.? Belvidera, and Calista, and Isabella, and Euphrasia, are they less liked than Imogen, or than Juliet, or than Desdemona?[18] Are they not spoken of and remembered in the same way? Is not the female performer as great (as they call it) in one as in the other? Did not Garrick shine, and was he not ambitious of shining in every drawling tragedy that his wretched day produced, – the productions of the Hills and the Murphys and

33

the Browns,[19] – and shall he have that honour to dwell in our minds for ever as an inseparable concomitant with Shakspeare? A kindred mind! O who can read that affecting sonnet of Shakspeare which alludes to his profession as a player: —

> Oh for my sake do you with Fortune chide,
> The guilty goddess of my harmful deeds,
> That did not better for my life provide
> Than public means which public custom [manners]
>   breeds—
> Thence comes it that my name receives a brand;
> And almost thence my nature is subdued
> To what it works in, like the dyer's hand—[20]

Or that other confession: —

> Alas! 'tis true, I have gone here and there,
> And made myself a motly to thy view,
> Gor'd mine own thoughts, sold cheap what is most
>   dear—[21]

Who can read these instances of jealous self-watchfulness in our sweet Shakspeare, and dream of any congeniality between him and one that, by every tradition of him, appears to have been as mere a player as ever existed; to have had his mind tainted with the lowest players' vices, – envy and jealousy, and miserable cravings after applause; one who in the exercise of his profession was jealous even of the women-performers that stood in his way; a manager full of managerial tricks and stratagems and finesse: that any resemblance should be dreamed of between him and Shakspeare, – Shakspeare who, in the plenitude and consciousness of his own powers, could with that noble modesty, which we can neither imitate nor appreciate, express himself thus of his own sense of his own defects: —

> Wishing me like to one more rich in hope,
> Featur'd like him, like him with friends possest;
> Desiring *this man's art, and that man's scope.*[22]

I am almost disposed to deny to Garrick the merit of being an admirer of Shakspeare. A true lover of his excellencies he certainly was not; for would any true lover of them have admitted into his matchless scenes such ribald trash as Tate and Cibber,[23] and the rest of them, that

With their darkness durst affront his light,[24]

have foisted into the acting plays of Shakspeare? I believe it impossible that he could have had a proper reverence for Shakspeare, and have condescended to go through that interpolated scene in Richard the Third, in which Richard tries to break his wife's heart by telling her he loves another woman, and says, 'if she survives this she is immortal.'[25] Yet I doubt not he delivered this vulgar stuff with as much anxiety of emphasis as any of the genuine parts; and for acting, it is as well calculated as any. But we have seen the part of Richard lately produce great fame to an actor by his manner of playing it, and it lets us into the secret of acting, and of popular judgments of Shakspeare derived from acting. Not one of the spectators who have witnessed Mr C.'s[26] exertions in that part, but has come away with a proper conviction that Richard is a very wicked man, and kills little children in their beds, with something like the pleasure which the giants and ogres in children's books are represented to have taken in that practice; moreover, that he is very close and shrewd and devilish cunning, for you could see that by his eye.

But is in fact this the impression we have in reading the Richard of Shakspeare? Do we feel any thing like disgust, as we do at that butcher-like representation of him that passes for him on the stage? A horror at his crimes blends with the effect which we feel, but how is it qualified, how is it carried off, by the rich intellect which he displays, his resources, his wit, his buoyant spirits, his vast knowledge and insight into characters, the poetry of his part, – not an atom of all which is made perceivable in Mr C.'s way of acting it. Nothing but his crimes, his actions, is visible; they are prominent and staring; the murderer stands out, but where is the lofty genius, the man of vast capacity, – the profound, the witty, accomplished Richard?

The truth is, the Characters of Shakspeare are so much the objects of meditation rather than of interest or curiosity as to their actions, that while we are reading any of his great criminal characters, – Macbeth, Richard, even Iago, – we think not so much of the crimes which they commit, as of the ambition, the aspiring spirit, the intellectual activity, which prompts them to overleap those moral fences. Barnwell is a wretched murderer; there is a certain fitness between his neck and the rope; he is the legitimate heir to the gallows; nobody who thinks at all can think of any alleviating circumstances in his case to make him a fit object of mercy. Or to take an instance from the higher tragedy, what else but a mere assassin is Glenalvon! [27] Do we think of any thing but of the crime which he commits, and the rack which he deserves? That is all which we really think about him. Whereas in corresponding characters in Shakspeare so little do the actions comparatively affect us, that while the impulses, the inner mind in all its perverted greatness, solely seems real and is exclusively attended to, the crime is comparatively nothing. But when we see these things represented, the acts which they do are comparatively every thing, their impulses nothing. The state of sublime emotion into which we are elevated by those images of night and horror which Macbeth is made to utter, that solemn prelude with which he entertains the time till the bell shall strike which is to call him to murder Duncan, – when we no longer read it in a book, when we have given up that vantage-ground of abstraction which reading possesses over seeing, and come to see a man in his bodily shape before our eyes actually preparing to commit a murder, if the acting be true and impressive, as I have witnessed it in Mr K.'s[28] performance of that part, the painful anxiety about the act, the natural longing to prevent it while it yet seems unperpetrated, the too close pressing semblance of reality, give a pain and an uneasiness which totally destroy all the delight which the words in the book convey, where the deed doing never presses upon us with the painful sense of presence: it rather seems to belong to history, – to something past and inevitable, if it has any thing to do with time at all. The sublime images, the poetry alone, is that which is present to our minds in the reading.

So to see Lear acted, – to see an old man tottering about the stage with a walking-stick, turned out of doors by his daughters in a rainy night, has nothing in it but what is painful and disgusting. We want to take him into shelter and relieve him. That is all the feeling which the acting of Lear ever produced in me. But the Lear of Shakspeare cannot be acted. The contemptible machinery by which they mimic the storm which he goes out in, is not more inadequate to represent the horrors of the real elements, than any actor can be to represent Lear: they might more easily propose to personate the Satan of Milton upon a stage, or one of Michael Angelo's terrible figures. The greatness of Lear is not in corporal dimension, but in intellectual: the explosions of his passion are terrible as a volcano: they are storms turning up and disclosing to the bottom that sea, his mind, with all its vast riches. It is his mind which is laid bare. This case of flesh and blood seems too insignificant to be thought on; even as he himself neglects it. On the stage we see nothing but corporal infirmities and weakness, the impotence of rage; while we read it, we see not Lear, but we are Lear, – we are in his mind, we are sustained by a grandeur which baffles the malice of daughters and storms; in the aberrations of his reason, we discover a mighty irregular power of reasoning, immethodized from the ordinary purposes of life, but exerting its powers, as the wind blows where it listeth, at will upon the corruptions and abuses of mankind. What have looks, or tones, to do with that sublime identification of his age with that of the *heavens themselves*, when in his reproaches to them for conniving at the injustice of his children, he reminds them that 'they themselves are old.'[29] What gesture shall we appropriate to this? What has the voice or the eye to do with such things? But the play is beyond all art, as the tamperings with it shew: it is too hard and stony; it must have love-scenes, and a happy ending. It is not enough that Cordelia is a daughter, she must shine as a lover too. Tate has put his hook in the nostrils of this Leviathan, for Garrick and his followers, the showmen of the scene, to draw the mighty beast about more easily. A happy ending! – as if the living martyrdom that Lear had gone through, – the flaying of his feelings alive, did not make a fair dismissal from the stage of life the only decorous thing for him. If he is to live and be happy after, if he could sustain this world's burden after, why all this pudder[30] and preparation, – why torment us with all this unnecessary sympathy? As if the childish pleasure of getting his gilt robes and sceptre again could tempt him to act over again his misused station, – as if at his years, and with his experience, any thing was left but to die.

Lear is essentially impossible to be represented on a stage. But how many dramatic personages are there in Shakspeare, which though more tractable and feasible (if I may so speak) than Lear, yet from some circumstance, some adjunct to their character, are improper to be shewn to our bodily eye. Othello for instance. Nothing can be more soothing, more flattering to the nobler parts of our natures, than to read of a young Venetian lady of highest extraction, through the force of love and from a sense of merit in him whom she loved, laying aside every consideration of kindred, and country, and colour, and wedding with a *coal-black Moor* – (for such he is represented, in the imperfect state of knowledge respecting foreign countries in those days, compared with our own, or in compliance with popular notions, though the Moors are now well enough known to be by many shades less unworthy of a white woman's fancy) – it is the perfect triumph of virtue over accidents, of the imagination over the senses. She sees Othello's colour in his mind. But upon the stage, when the imagination is no longer the ruling faculty, but we are left to our poor unassisted senses, I appeal to every one that has seen Othello played, whether he did not, on the contrary, sink Othello's mind in his colour; whether he did not find something extremely revolting in the courtship and wedded caresses of Othello and Desdemona; and whether the actual sight of the thing did not over-weigh all that beautiful compromise which we make in reading; – and the reason it should do so is obvious, because there is just so much reality presented to our senses as to give a perception of disagreement, with not enough of belief in the internal motives, – all that which is unseen, – to overpower and reconcile the first and obvious prejudices.* What we see upon a stage is body and bodily action; what we are conscious of in reading is almost exclusively the mind, and its movements: and this I think may sufficiently account for the very different sort of delight with which the same play so often affects us in the reading and the seeing.

It requires little reflection to perceive, that if those characters in Shakspeare which are within the precincts of nature, have yet something in them which appeals too exclusively to the imagination, to admit of their being made objects to the senses without suffering a change and a diminution, – that still stronger the objec-

---

*The error of supposing that because Othello's colour does not offend us in the reading, it should also not offend us in the seeing, is just such a fallacy as supposing that an Adam and Eve in a picture shall affect us just as they do in the poem. But in the poem we for a while have Paradisaical senses given us, which vanish when we see a man and his wife without clothes in the picture. The painters themselves feel this, as is apparent by the awkward shifts they have recourse to, to make them look not quite naked; by a sort of prophetic anachronism, antedating the invention of fig-leaves. So in the reading of the play, we see with Desdemona's eyes; in the seeing of it, we are forced to look with our own. [Lamb's note]

tion must lie against representing another line of characters, which Shakspeare has introduced to give a wildness and a supernatural elevation to his scenes, as if to remove them still farther from that assimilation to common life in which their excellence is vulgarly supposed to consist. When we read the incantations of those terrible beings the Witches in Macbeth, though some of the ingredients of their hellish composition savour of the grotesque, yet is the effect upon us other than the most serious and appalling that can be imagined? Do we not feel spell-bound as Macbeth was? Can any mirth accompany a sense of their presence? We might as well laugh under a consciousness of the principle of Evil himself being truly and really present with us. But attempt to bring these beings on to a stage, and you turn them instantly into so many old women, that men and children are to laugh at. Contrary to the old saying, that 'seeing is believing,' the sight actually destroys the faith; and the mirth in which we indulge at their expense, when we see these creatures upon a stage, seems to be a sort of indemnification which we make to ourselves for the terror which they put us in when reading made them an object of belief, – when we surrendered up our reason to the poet, as children to their nurses and their elders; and we laugh at our fears, as children who thought they saw something in the dark, triumph when the bringing in of a candle discovers the vanity of their fears. For this exposure of super-natural agents upon a stage is truly bringing in a candle to expose their own delusiveness. It is the solitary taper and the book that generates a faith in these terrors: a ghost by chandelier light, and in good company, deceives no spectators, – a ghost that can be measured by the eye, and his human dimensions made out at leisure. The sight of a well-lighted house,[31] and a well-dressed audience, shall arm the most nervous child against any apprehensions: as Tom Brown says of the impenetrable skin of Achilles with his impenetrable armour over it, 'Bully Dawson would have fought the devil with such advantages.'[32]

Much has been said, and deservedly, in reprobation of the vile mixture which Dryden has thrown into the Tempest:[33] doubtless without some such vicious alloy, the impure ears of that age would never have sate out to hear so much innocence of love as is contained in the sweet courtship of Ferdinand and Miranda. But is the Tempest of Shakspeare at all a subject for stage representation? It is one thing to read of an enchanter, and to believe the wondrous tale while we are reading it; but to have a conjuror brought before us in his conjuring-gown, with his spirits about him, which none but himself and some hundred of favoured spectators before the curtain are supposed to see, involves such a quantity of the *hateful incredible*, that all our reverence for the author cannot hinder us from perceiving such gross attempts upon the senses to be in the highest degree childish and inefficient. Spirits and fairies cannot be represented, they cannot even be painted, – they can only be believed. But the elaborate and anxious provision of scenery, which the luxury of the age demands, in these cases works a quite contrary effect to what is intended. That which in comedy, or plays of familiar life, adds so much to the life of the imitation, in plays which appeal to the higher faculties, positively destroys the illusion which it is introduced to aid. A parlour or a drawing-room, – a library opening into a garden, – a garden with an alcove in it, – a street, or the piazza of Covent-garden, does well enough in a scene; we are content to give as much credit to it as it demands; or rather, we think little about it, – it is little more than reading at the top of a page, 'Scene, a Garden;' we do not imagine ourselves there, but we readily admit the imitation of familiar objects. But to think by the help of painted trees and caverns, which we know to be painted, to transport our minds to Prospero, and his island and his lonely cell;* or by the aid of a fiddle dexterously thrown in, in an interval of speaking, to make us believe that we hear those supernatural noises of which the isle was full: – the Orrery Lecturer at the Haymarket[34] might as well hope, by his musical glasses cleverly stationed out of sight behind his apparatus, to make us believe that we do indeed hear the chrystal spheres ring out that chime, which if it were to inwrap our fancy long, Milton thinks,

> Time would run back and fetch the age of gold,
> And speckled vanity
> Would sicken soon and die,
> And leprous Sin would melt from earthly mould;
> Yea Hell itself would pass away,
> And leave its dolorous mansions to the peering day.[35]

---

*It will be said these things are done in pictures. But pictures and scenes are very different things. Painting is a world of itself, but in scene-painting there is the attempt to deceive; and there is the discordancy, never to be got over, between painted scenes and real people. [Lamb's note]

The Garden of Eden, with our first parents in it, is not more impossible to be shewn on a stage, than the Enchanted Isle, with its no less interesting and innocent first settlers.

The subject of Scenery is closely connected with that of the Dresses, which are so anxiously attended to on our stage. I remember the last time I saw Macbeth played, the discrepancy I felt at the changes of garment which he varied, – the shiftings and re-shiftings, like a Romish priest at mass. The luxury of stage-improvements, and the importunity of the public eye, require this. The coronation robe of the Scottish monarch was fairly a counter-part to that which our King wears when he goes to the Parliament-house, – just so full and cumbersome, and set out with ermine and pearls. And if things must be represented, I see not what to find fault with in this. But in reading, what robe are we conscious of? Some dim images of royalty – a crown and sceptre, may float before our eyes, but who shall describe the fashion of it? Do we see in our mind's eye what Webb[36] or any other robe-maker could pattern? This is the inevitable consequence of imitating every thing, to make all things natural. Whereas the reading of a tragedy is a fine abstraction. It presents to the fancy just so much of external appearances as to make us feel that we are among flesh and blood, while by far the greater and better part of our imagination is employed upon the thoughts and internal machinery of the character. But in acting, scenery, dress, the most contemptible things, call upon us to judge of their naturalness.

Perhaps it would be no bad similitude, to liken the pleasure which we take in seeing one of these fine plays acted, compared with that quiet delight which we find in the reading of it, to the different feelings with which a reviewer, and a man that is not a reviewer, reads a fine poem. The accursed critical habit, – the being called upon to judge and pronounce, must make it quite a different thing to the former. In seeing these plays acted, we are affected just as judges. When Hamlet compares the two pictures of Gertrude's first and second husband, who wants to see the pictures? But in the acting, a miniature must be lugged out; which we know not to be the picture, but only to shew how finely a miniature may be represented. This shewing of every thing, levels all things: it makes tricks, bows, and curtesies, of importance. Mrs. S.[37] never got more fame by any thing than by the manner in which she dismisses the guests in the banquet-scene in Macbeth: it is as much remembered as any of her thrilling tones or impressive looks. But does such a trifle as this enter into the imaginations of the readers of that wild and wonderful scene? Does not the mind dismiss the feasters as rapidly as it can? Does it care about the gracefulness of the doing it? But by acting, and judging of acting, all these non-essentials are raised into an importance, injurious to the main interest of the play.

I have confined my observations to the tragic parts of Shakspeare. It would be no very difficult task to extend the enquiry to his comedies; and to shew why Falstaff, Shallow, Sir Hugh Evans,[38] and the rest, are equally incompatible with stage representation. The length to which this Essay has run, will make it, I am afraid, sufficiently distasteful to the Amateurs of the Theatre, without going any deeper into the subject at present.

On the Tragedies of Shakspeare, 1811

I was pleased with the reply of a gentleman, who being asked which book he esteemed most in his library, answered, – 'Shakspeare': being asked which he esteemed next best, replied, – 'Hogarth'. His graphic representations are indeed books: they have the teeming, fruitful, suggestive meaning of *words*. Other pictures we look at, – his prints we read.

In pursuance of this parallel, I have sometimes entertained myself with comparing the *Timon of Athens* of Shakspeare . . . and Hogarth's *Rake's Progress* together. The story, the moral, in both is nearly the same. The wild course of riot and extravagance, ending in the one with driving the Prodigal from the society of men into the solitude of the deserts, and in the other with conducting the Rake through his several stages of dissipation into the still more complete desolations of the mad-house, in the play and in the picture are described with almost equal force and nature. The levee of the Rake, which forms the subject of the second plate in the series, is almost a transcript of Timon's levee in the opening scene of that play. We find a dedicating poet, and other similar characters, in both.

The concluding scene in the *Rake's Progress* is perhaps superior to the last scenes of *Timon*. If we seek for something of kindred excellence in poetry, it must be in the scenes of Lear's beginning madness, where the King and the Fool and the Tom-o'Bedlam conspire to produce such a medley of mirth checked by misery, and misery rebuked by mirth; where the society of those 'strange bed-fellows'³⁹ which misfortunes have brought Lear acquainted with, so finely sets forth the destitute state of the monarch, while the lunatic bans of the one, and the disjointed sayings and wild but pregnant allusions of the other, so wonderfully sympathize with that confusion, which they seem to assist in the production of, in the senses of that 'child-changed father'.⁴⁰

In the scene in Bedlam, which terminates the *Rake's Progress*, we find the same assortment of the ludicrous with the terrible. Here is desperate madness, the overturning of originally strong thinking faculties, at which we shudder, as we contemplate the duration and pressure of affliction which it must have asked to destroy such a building; – and here is the gradual hurtless lapse into idiocy, of faculties, which at their best of times never having been strong, we look upon the consummation of their decay with no more of pity than is consistent with a smile. The mad taylor, the poor driveller that has gone out of his wits (and truly he appears to have had no great journey to go to get past their confines) for the love of *Charming Betty Careless*,⁴¹ – these half-laughable, scarce-pitiable objects take off from the horror which the principal figure would of itself raise, at the same time that they assist the feeling of the scene by contributing to the general notion of its subject: —

> Madness, thou chaos of the brain,
> What art thou, that pleasure giv'st and pain?
> Tyranny of Fancy's reign!
> Mechanic Fancy, that can build
> Vast labyrinths and mazes wild,
> With rule disjointed, shapeless measure,
> Fill'd with horror, fill'd with pleasure!
> Shapes of horror, that would even
> Cast doubts of mercy upon heaven.
> Shapes of pleasure, that, but seen,
> Would split the shaking sides of spleen.*

Is it carrying the spirit of comparison to excess to remark, that in the poor kneeling weeping female, who accompanies her seducer in his sad decay, there is something analogous to Kent, or Caius, as he delights rather to be called, in *Lear*, – the noblest pattern of virtue which even Shakspeare has conceived, – who follows his

*Lines inscribed under the plate. [Lamb's note]

The Rake's Progress. Plate VIII. The Rake in a Madhouse, by William Hogarth.

royal master in banishment, that had pronounced *his* banishment, and forgetful at once of his wrongs and dignities, taking on himself the disguise of a menial, retains his fidelity to the figure, his loyalty to the carcass, the shadow, the shell and empty husk of Lear?

. . . This [the Bedlam scene of the *Rake's Progress*] is high tragic painting, and we might as well deny to Shakspeare the honours of a great tragedian, because he has interwoven scenes of mirth with the serious business of his plays, as refuse to Hogarth the same praise for the concluding scenes of the *Rake's Progress*, because of the Comic Lunatics which he has thrown into the one, or the Alchymist that he has introduced in the other, who is paddling in the coals of his furnace, keeping alive the flames of vain hope within the very walls of the prison to which the vanity has conducted him, which have taught the darker lesson of extinguished hope to the desponding figure who is the principal person of the scene.

It is the force of these kindly admixtures, which assimilates the scenes of Hogarth and of Shakspeare to the drama of real life, where no such thing as pure tragedy is to be found; but merriment and infelicity, ponderous crime and featherlight vanity, like twiformed births, disagreeing complexions of one intertexture, perpetually unite to shew forth motley spectacles to the world. Then it is that the poet or painter shews his art, when in the selection of these comic adjuncts he chooses such circumstances as shall relieve, contrast with, or fall into, without forming a violent opposition to, his principal object. Who sees not that the Gravedigger in *Hamlet*, the Fool in *Lear*, have a kind of correspondency to, and fall in with, the subjects which they seem to interrupt, while the comic stuff in *Venice Preserved*, and the doggrel nonsense of the Cook and his poisoning associates in the *Rollo* of Beaumont and Fletcher,[42] are pure, irrelevant, impertinent discords, – as bad as the quarreling dog and cat under the table of the *Lord and the Disciples at Emmaus* of Titian? . . . It is worthy of observation, that he has seldom drawn a mean or insignificant countenance. Hogarth's mind was eminently reflective; and, as it has been well observed of Shakspeare, that he has transfused his own poetical character into the persons of his drama (they are all more or less *poets*) Hogarth has impressed a *thinking character* upon the persons of his canvas.

From *On the Genius and Character of Hogarth*, 1811.

> *Lear* Who are you?
> Mine eyes are not o' the best: I'll tell you straight
> . . . Are you not Kent?
> *Kent* The same;
> Your servant Kent. Where is your servant Caius?
> *Lear* He's a good fellow, I can tell you that;
> He'll strike, and quickly too: he's dead and rotten.
> *Kent* No, my good Lord; I am the very man—
> *Lear* I'll see that straight—
> *Kent* That from your first of difference and decay,
> Have follow'd your sad steps.
> *Lear* You are welcome hither. . . .
> *Albany* He knows not what he says; and vain it is
> That we present us to him.
> *Edgar* Look up, my Lord.
> *Kent* Vex not his ghost. O, let him pass! He hates him
>   much
> That would upon the rack of this rough world
> Stretch him out longer.[43]

So ends 'King Lear', the most stupendous of the Shakspearian dramas; and Kent, the noblest feature of the conceptions of his divine mind. This is the magnanimity of authorship when a writer, having a topic presented to him, fruitful of beauties for common minds, waives his privilege, and trusts to the judicious few for understanding the reason of his abstinence. What a pudder[44] would a common dramatist have raised here of a reconciliation scene, a perfect recognition, between the assumed Caius and his master! – to the suffusing of many fair eyes, and the moistening of cambric handkerchiefs. The old dying king partially catching at the truth, and immediately lapsing into obliviousness, with the high-minded carelessness of the other to have his services appreciated, as one that

> – served not for gain,
> Or follow'd out of form,[45]

are among the most judicious, not to say heart-touching, strokes in Shakspeare.

(from Table-Talk by the Late Elia, 1833)

So far from the position holding true, that great wit (or genius, in our modern way of speaking), has a necessary alliance with insanity,[46] the greatest wits, on the contrary, will ever be found to be the sanest writers. It is impossible for the mind to conceive of a mad Shakspeare. The greatness of wit, by which the poetic talent is here chiefly to be understood, manifests itself in the admirable balance of all the faculties. Madness is the disproportionate straining or excess of any one of them. 'So strong a wit,' says Cowley, speaking of a poetical friend,

> '– did Nature to him frame,
> As all things but his judgment overcame,
> His judgment like the heavenly moon did show,
> Tempering that mighty sea below.'[47]

The ground of the mistake is, that men, finding in the raptures of the higher poetry a condition of exaltation, to which they have no parallel in their own experience, besides the spurious resemblance of it in dreams and fevers, impute a state of dreaminess and fever to the poet. But the true poet dreams being awake. He is not possessed by his subject, but has dominion over it. In the groves of Eden he walks familiar as in his native paths. He ascends the empyrean heaven, and is not intoxicated. He treads the burning marl without dismay; he wins his flight without self-loss through realms of chaos 'and old night'.[48] Or if, abandoning himself to that severer chaos of a 'human mind untuned,'[49] he is content awhile to be mad with Lear, or to hate mankind (a sort of madness) with Timon, neither is that madness, nor this misanthropy, so unchecked, but that, – never letting the reins of reason wholly go, while most he seems to do so, – he has his better genius still whispering at his ear, with the good servant Kent suggesting saner counsels, or with the honest steward Flavius recommending kindlier resolutions. Where he seems most to recede from humanity, he will be found the truest to it. From beyond the scope of Nature if he summon possible existences, he subjugates them to the law of her consistency. He is beautifully loyal to that sovereign directress, even when he appears most to betray and desert her. His ideal tribes submit to policy; his very monsters are tamed to his hand, even as that wild sea-brood, shepherded by Proteus.[50] He tames, and he clothes them with attributes of flesh and blood, till they wonder at themselves, like Indian Islanders

47

forced to submit to European vesture. Caliban, the Witches, are as true to the laws of their own nature (ours with a difference), as Othello, Hamlet and Macbeth.

(from 'Sanity of True Genius,' *Last Essays of Elia*, 1833)

Lamb spoke well about Shakespeare. I had objected to Coleridge's assertion that Shakespeare, as it were, identified himself with everything except the vicious; and I observed that if Shakespeare's *becoming* a character is to be determined by the truth and vivacity of his delineation, he had *become* some of the vicious characters as well as the virtuous. Lamb justified Coleridge's remark, by saying that Shakespeare never gives characters wholly odious and detestable. I advanced the King in *Hamlet* as altogether mean; and he allowed this to be the worst of Shakespeare's characters. He has not another like it. I cited Lady Macbeth. 'I think this one of Shakespeare's worst characters,' said Lamb. 'It is also inconsistent with itself. Her sleep-walking does not suit so hardened a being.' It occurs to me, however, that this very sleep-walking is, perhaps, the vindication of Shakespeare's portraiture of the character, as thereby the honour of human nature, if I may use the expression, is saved. The *voluntary* actions and sentiments of Lady Macbeth are all inhuman, but her *involuntary* nature rises up against her habitual feelings, which sprang out of depraved passions. Hence, though while awake she is a monster, she is a woman in her sleep. I then referred to the Bastard in 'Lear', but Lamb considered his character as the result of provocation on account of his illegitimacy. Lamb mentioned Iago and Richard III as admirable illustrations of the skill with which Shakespeare could make his worst characters interesting. I noticed King John and Lewis, as if Shakespeare meant, like a Jacobin, to show how base kings are. Lamb did not remark on this, but said, ' "King John" is one of the plays I like least.' He praised 'Richard II'.

H. C. Robinson's notes of a conservation.

It is the praise of Shakspeare, with reference to the play-writers, his contemporaries, that he has so few revolting characters. Yet he has one that is singularly mean and disagreeable – the King in Hamlet. Neither has he characters of insignificance, unless the phantom that stalks over the stage as Julius Caesar, in the play of that name, may be accounted one. Neither has he envious characters, excepting the short part of Don John, in Much Ado About Nothing. Neither has he unentertaining characters, if we except Parolles, and the little that there is of the Clown, in All's Well that Ends Well.

It would settle the dispute, as to whether Shakspeare intended Othello for a jealous character, to consider how differently we are affected towards him, and for Leontes in the Winter's Tale. Leontes *is* that character. Othello's fault was simply credulity.

Is it possible that Shakspeare should never have read Homer, in Chapman's version[51] at least? If he had read it, could he mean to *travesty* it in the parts of those big boobies, Ajax and Achilles? Ulysses, Nestor and Agamemnon, are true to their parts in the Iliad: they are gentlemen at least. Thersites, though unamusing, is fairly deducible from it. Troilus and Cressida are a fine graft upon it. But those two big bulks— . . .

From Table-Talk by the Late Elia, 1833

III The Comedies

At the end of the 'Reflector' version of the essay 'On the Tragedies of Shakspeare', Lamb wrote: 'I have hitherto confined my observation to the Tragic part of Shakspeare; in some future number I propose to extend this inquiry to the Comedies.' Unfortunately 'The Reflector' folded with the fourth number and Lamb never took up the proposed subject. When he reprinted the essay for the 'Works' he reworded the reference, merely stating that it would be easy to apply to the comedies the same argument of unfitness for stage representation.

One may regret that Lamb, with his keen sense of humour and sharp wit, did not write more about Shakespeare's comedies. His one long consideration of a comedy formed part of a series of articles for the 'London Magazine' of 1822, entitled 'The Old Actors.' The material was rearranged for inclusion in the Elia book and the present essay of the same title is one section of the original.

Where the commentary on 'Twelfth Night' exploits Lamb's long familiarity with the stage, the remarks on 'The Tempest' and 'Measure for Measure' demonstrate his more scholarly approach to the text. Lamb's interest in old books made him sensitive to Elizabethan English and to the nuances of Shakespeare's language. Even in his whimsical essays, Lamb occasionally incorporates a sharp critical observation, as in his noting of the inconsistency in a passage from 'Measure for Measure.'

The casual sight of an old Play Bill, which I picked up the other day – I know not by what chance it was preserved so long – tempts me to call to mind a few of the Players, who make the principal figure in it. It presents the cast of parts in the Twelfth Night, at the old Drury-lane Theatre two-and-thirty years ago.[1] There is something very touching in these old remembrances. They make us think how we *once* used to read a Play Bill – not, as now peradventure, singling out a favorite performer, and casting a negligent eye over the rest; but spelling out every name, down to the very mutes and servants of the scene; – when it was a matter of no small moment to us whether Whitfield, or Packer, took the part of Fabian; when

Benson, and Burton, and Phillimore[2] – names of small account – had an importance, beyond what we can be content to attribute now to the time's best actors. – 'Orsino, by Mr Barrymore.' – What a full Shakspearian sound it carries! how fresh to memory arise the image, and the manner, of the gentle actor!

Those who have only seen Mrs Jordan within the last ten or fifteen years, can have no adequate notion of her performance of such parts as Ophelia; Helena, in All's Well that Ends Well; and Viola in this play. Her voice had latterly acquired a coarseness, which suited well enough with her Nells and Hoydens,[3] but in those days it sank, with her steady melting eye, into the heart. Her joyous parts – in which her memory now chiefly lives – in her youth were outdone by her plaintive ones. There is no giving an account how she delivered the disguised story of her love for Orsino. It was no set speech, that she had foreseen, so as to weave it into an harmonious period, line necessarily following line, to make up the music – yet I have heard it so spoken, or rather *read*, not without its grace and beauty – but, when she had declared her sister's history to be a 'blank,' and that she 'never told her love,' there was a pause, as if the story had ended – and then the image of the 'worm in the bud' came up as a new suggestion – and the heightened image of 'Patience' still followed after that, as by some growing (and not mechanical) process, thought springing up after thought, I would almost say, as they were watered by her tears. So in those fine lines—

> Write loyal canto[n]s of contemned love—
> Hollow your name to the reverberate hills—[4]

there was no preparation made in the foregoing image for that which was to follow. She used no rhetoric in her passion; or it was nature's own rhetoric, most legitimate then, when it seemed altogether without rule or law.

Mrs Powel (now Mrs Renard),[5] then in the pride of her beauty, made an admirable Olivia. She was particularly excellent in her unbending scenes in conversation with the Clown. I have seen some Olivias – and those very sensible actresses too – who in these interlocutions have seemed to set their wits at the jester, and to vie conceits with him in downright emulation. But she used him for her sport, like what he was, to trifle a leisure sentence or two with, and then to be dismissed, and she to be the Great Lady

51

still. She touched the imperious fantastic humour of the character with nicety. Her fine spacious person filled the scene.

The part of Malvolio has in my judgment been so often misunderstood, and the *general merits* of the actor, who then played it, so unduly appreciated, that I shall hope for pardon, if I am a little prolix upon these points.

Of all the actors who flourished in my time – a melancholy phrase if taken aright, reader – Bensley[6] had most of the swell of soul, was greatest in the delivery of heroic conceptions, the emotions consequent upon the presentment of a great idea to the fancy. He had the true poetical enthusiasm – the rarest faculty among players. None that I remember possessed even a portion of that fine madness which he threw out in Hotspur's famous rant about glory, or the transports of the Venetian incendiary at the vision of the fired city.[7] His voice had the dissonance, and at times the inspiriting effect of the trumpet. His gait was uncouth and stiff, but no way embarrassed by affectation; and the thorough-bred gentleman was uppermost in every movement. He seized the moment of passion with the greatest truth; like a faithful clock, never striking before the time; never anticipating or leading you to anticipate. He was totally destitute of trick and artifice. He seemed come upon the stage to do the poet's message simply, and he did it with as genuine fidelity as the nuncios in Homer deliver the errands of the gods. He let the passion or the sentiment do its own work without prop or bolstering. He would have scorned to mountebank it; and betrayed none of that *cleverness* which is the bane of serious acting. For this reason, his Iago was the only endurable one which I remember to have seen. No spectator from his action could divine more of his artifice than Othello was supposed to do. His confessions in soliloquy alone put you in possession of the mystery. There were no by-intimations to make the audience fancy their own discernment so much greater than that of the Moor – who commonly stands like a great helpless mark set up for mine Ancient, and a quantity of barren spectators, to shoot their bolts at. The Iago of Bensley did not go to work so grossly. There was a triumphant tone about the character, natural to a general consciousness of power; but none of that petty vanity which chuckles and cannot contain itself upon any little successful stroke of its knavery – as is common with your small villains, and green probationers in mischief. It did not clap or crow before its time. It was not a man setting his wits at a child, and winking all the while at other children who are mightily pleased at being let into the secret; but a consummate villain entrapping a noble nature into toils, against which no discernment was available, where the manner was as fathomless as the purpose seemed dark, and without motive. The part of Malvolio, in the Twelfth Night, was performed by Bensley, with a richness and a dignity, of which (to judge from some recent castings of that character) the very tradition must be worn out from the stage. No manager in those days would have dreamed of giving it to Mr Baddeley, or Mr Parsons: when Bensley was occasionally absent from the theatre, John Kemble[8] thought it no derogation to succeed to the part. Malvolio is not essentially ludicrous. He becomes comic but by accident. He is cold, austere, repelling; but dignified, consistent, and, for what appears, rather of an over-stretched morality. Maria describes him as a sort of Puritan; and he might have worn his gold chain with honour in one of our old round-head families, in the service of a Lambert, or a Lady Fairfax.[9] But his morality and his manners are misplaced in Illyria. He is opposed to the proper *levities* of the piece, and falls in the unequal contest. Still his pride, or his gravity, (call it which you will) is inherent, and native to the man, not mock or affected, which latter only are the fit objects to excite laughter. His quality is at the best unlovely, but neither buffoon nor contemptible. His bearing is lofty, a little above his station, but probably not much above his deserts. We see no reason why he should not have been brave, honourable, accomplished. His careless committal of the ring to the ground (which he was commissioned to restore to Cesario), bespeaks a generosity of birth and feeling. His dialect on all occasions is that of a gentleman, and a man of education. We must not confound him with the eternal old, low steward of comedy. He is master of the household to a great Princess;[10] a dignity probably conferred upon him for other respects than age or length of service. Olivia, at the first indication of his supposed madness, declares that she 'would not have him miscarry for half of her dowry.' Does this look as if the character was meant to appear little or insignificant? Once, indeed, she accuses him to his face – of what? – of being 'sick of self-love,' – but with a gentleness and considerateness which could not have been, if she had not thought that this particular infirmity shaded some virtues. His rebuke to the knight, and his sottish revellers, is sensible and spirited; and when

Robert Bensley as Hubert (left), with Powell as King John, from a painting by J. H. Mortimer.

we take into consideration the unprotected condition of his
mistress, and the strict regard with which her state of real or
dissembled mourning would draw the eyes of the world upon her
house-affairs, Malvolio might feel the honour of the family in
some sort in his keeping; as it appears not that Olivia had any more
brothers, or kinsmen, to look to it – for Sir Toby had dropped all
such nice respects at the buttery hatch. That Malvolio was meant
to be represented as possessing estimable qualities, the expression
of the Duke in his anxiety to have him reconciled, almost infers.
'Pursue him, and entreat him to a peace.'[11] Even in his abused state
of chains and darkness, a sort of greatness seems never to desert
him. He argues highly and well with the supposed Sir Topas, and
philosophises gallantly upon his straw.* There must have been
some shadow of worth about the man; he must have been something more than a mere vapour – a thing of straw, or Jack in
office – before Fabian and Maria could have ventured sending him
upon a courting–errand to Olivia. There was some consonancy (as
he would say) in the undertaking, or the jest would have been too
bold even for that house of misrule.

Bensley, accordingly, threw over the part an air of Spanish
loftiness. He looked, spake, and moved like an old Castilian. He
was starch, spruce, opinionated, but his superstructure of pride
seemed bottomed upon a sense of worth. There was something in
it beyond the coxcomb. It was big and swelling, but you could not
be sure that it was hollow. You might wish to see it taken down,
but you felt that it was upon an elevation. He was magnificent from
the outset; but when the decent sobrieties of the character began
to give way, and the poison of self-love, in his conceit of the
Countess's affection, gradually to work, you would have thought
that the hero of La Mancha[12] in person stood before you. How he
went smiling to himself! with what ineffable carelessness would he
twirl his gold chain! what a dream it was! you were infected with
the illusion, and did not wish that it should be removed! you had
no room for laughter! if an unseasonable reflection of morality
obtruded itself, it was a deep sense of the pitiable infirmity of

Clown. What is the opinion of Pythagoras concerning wild fowl?
Mal. That the soul of our grandam might haply inhabit a bird.
Clown. What thinkest thou of his opinion?
Mal. I think nobly of the soul, and no way approve of his opinion.
[Lamb's note. See IV. ii. 48-54]

man's nature, that can lay him open to such frenzies – but in truth you rather admired than pitied the lunacy while it lasted – you felt that an hour of such mistake was worth an age with the eyes open. Who would not wish to live but for a day in the conceit of such a lady's love as Olivia? Why, the Duke would have given his principality but for a quarter of a minute, sleeping or waking, to have been so deluded. The man seemed to tread upon air, to taste manna, to walk with his head in the clouds, to mate Hyperion.[13] O! shake not the castles of his pride – endure yet for a season bright moments of confidence – 'stand still ye watches of the element,'[14] that Malvolio may be still in fancy fair Olivia's lord – but fate and retribution say no – I hear the mischievous titter of Maria – the witty taunts of Sir Toby – the still more insupportable triumph of the foolish knight – the counterfeit Sir Topas is unmasked – and 'thus the whirligig of time,' as the true clown hath it, 'brings in his revenges.'[15] I confess that I never saw the catastrophe of this character, while Bensley played it, without a kind of tragic interest. There was good foolery too. Few now remember Dodd.[16] What an Aguecheek the stage lost in him! Lovegrove,[17] who came nearest to the old actors, revived the character some few seasons ago, and made it sufficiently grotesque; but Dodd was *it*, as it came out of nature's hands. It might be said to remain *in puris naturalibus*.[18] In expressing slowness of apprehension this actor surpassed all others. You could see the first dawn of an idea stealing slowly over his countenance, climbing up by little and little, with a painful process, till it cleared up at last to the fulness of a twilight conception – its highest meridian. He seemed to keep back his intellect, as some have had the power to retard their pulsation. The balloon takes less time in filling, than it took to cover the expansion of his broad moony face over all its quarters with expression. A glimmer of understanding would appear in a corner of his eye, and for lack of fuel go out again. A part of his forehead would catch a little intelligence, and be a long time in communicating it to the remainder.

I am ill at dates, but I think it is now better than five and twenty years ago that walking in the gardens of Gray's Inn – they were then far finer than they are now – the accursed Verulam Buildings had not encroached upon all the east side of them, cutting out delicate green crankles, and shouldering away one of two of the stately alcoves of the terrace – the survivor stands gaping and relationless as if it remembered its brother – they are still the best gardens of any of the Inns of Court, my beloved Temple[19] not forgotten – have the gravest character, their aspect being altogether reverend and law-breathing – Bacon has left the impress of his foot upon their gravel walks – taking my afternoon solace on a summer day upon the aforesaid terrace, a comely sad personage came towards me, whom, from his grave air and deportment, I judged to be one of the old Benchers of the Inn. He had a serious thoughtful forehead, and seemed to be in meditations of mortality. As I have an instinctive awe of old Benchers, I was passing him with that sort of sub-indicative token of respect which one is apt to demonstrate towards a venerable stranger, and which rather denotes an inclination to greet him, than any positive motion of the body to that effect – a species of humility and will-worship which I observe, nine times out of ten, rather puzzles than pleases the person it is offered to – when the face turning full upon me strangely identified itself with that of Dodd. Upon close inspection I was not mistaken. But could this sad thoughtful countenance be the same vacant face of folly which I had hailed so often under circumstances of gaiety; which I had never seen without a smile, or recognised but as the usher of mirth; that looked out so formally flat in Foppington, so frothily pert in Tattle, so impotently busy in Backbite; so blankly divested of all meaning, or resolutely expressive of none, in Acres, in Fribble,[20] and a thousand agreeable impertinences? Was this the face – full of thought and carefulness – that had so often divested itself at will of every trace of either to give me diversion, to clear my cloudy face for two or three hours at least of its furrows? Was this the face – manly, sober, intelligent, – which I had so often despised, made mocks at, made merry with? The remembrance of the freedoms which I had taken with it came upon me with a reproach of insult. I could have asked it pardon. I thought it looked upon me with a sense of injury. There is something strange as well as sad in seeing actors – your pleasant fellows particularly – subjected to and suffering the common lot – their fortunes, their casualties, their deaths, seem to belong to the scene, their actions to be amenable to poetic justice only. We can hardly connect them with more awful responsibilities. The death of this fine actor took place shortly after this meeting. He had quitted the stage some months; and, as I learned afterwards, had been in the habit of resorting daily to these gardens almost to the day of his

57

decease. In these serious walks probably he was divesting himself of many scenic and some real vanities – weaning himself from the frivolities of the lesser and the greater theatre – doing gentle penance for a life of no very reprehensible fooleries, – taking off by degrees the buffoon mask which he might feel he had worn too long – and rehearsing for a more solemn cast of part. Dying he 'put on the weeds of Dominic.'*[21]

If few can remember Dodd, many yet living will not easily forget the pleasant creature, who in those days enacted the part of the Clown to Dodd's Sir Andrew. – Richard, or rather Dicky Suett[22] – for so in his life-time he delighted to be called, and time hath ratified the appellation – lieth buried on the north side of the cemetery of Holy Paul, to whose service his nonage and tender years were dedicated.[23] There are who do yet remember him at that period – his pipe clear and harmonious. He would often speak of his chorister days, when he was 'cherub Dicky.'

What clipped his wings, or made it expedient that he should exchange the holy for the profane state; whether he had lost his good voice (his best recommendation to that office), like Sir John, 'with hallooing and singing of anthems;'[24] or whether he was adjudged to lack something, even in those early years, of the gravity indispensable to an occupation which professeth to 'commerce with the skies'[25] – I could never rightly learn; but we find him, after the probation of a twelvemonth or so, reverting to a secular condition, and become one of us.

I think he was not altogether of that timber, out of which cathedral seats and sounding boards are hewed. But if a glad heart – kind and therefore glad – be any part of sanctity, then might the robe of Motley, with which he invested himself with so much humility after his deprivation, and which he wore so long with so much blameless satisfaction to himself and to the public, be accepted for a surplice – his white stole, and *albe*.

*Dodd was a man of reading, and left at his death a choice collection of old English literature. I should judge him to have been a man of wit. I know one instance of an impromptu which no length of study could have bettered. My merry friend, Jem White, had seen him one evening in Aguecheek, and recognising Dodd the next day in Fleet Street, was irresistibly impelled to take off his hat and salute him as the identical Knight of the preceding evening with a 'Save you, *Sir Andrew*.' Dodd, not at all disconcerted at this unusual address from a stranger, with a courteous half-rebuking wave of the hand, put him off with an 'Away, *Fool*.' [Lamb's note.]

The first fruits of his secularization was an engagement upon the boards of Old Drury, at which theatre he commenced, as I have been told, with adopting the manner of Parsons[26] in old men's characters. At the period in which most of us knew him, he was no more an imitator than he was in any true sense himself imitable.

He was the Robin Good-Fellow of the stage. He came in to trouble all things with a welcome perplexity, himself no whit troubled for the matter. He was known, like Puck, by his note – *Ha! Ha! Ha!* – sometimes deepening to *Ho! Ho! Ho!* with an irresistible accession, derived perhaps remotely from his ecclesiastical education, foreign to his prototype of, – *O La!* Thousands of hearts yet respond to the chuckling *O La!* of Dicky Suett, brought back to their remembrance by the faithful transcript of his friend Mathews's mimicry.[27] The 'force of nature could no further go.'[28] He drolled upon the stock of these two syllables richer than the cuckoo.

Care, that troubles all the world, was forgotten in his composition. Had he had but two grains (nay, half a grain) of it, he could never have supported himself upon those two spider's strings, which served him (in the latter part of his unmixed existence) as legs. A doubt or a scruple must have made him totter, a sigh have puffed him down; the weight of a frown had staggered him, a wrinkle made him lose his balance. But on he went, scrambling upon those airy stilts of his, with Robin Good-Fellow, 'thorough brake, thorough briar,'[29] reckless of a scratched face or a torn doublet.

Shakspeare foresaw him, when he framed his fools and jesters. They have all the true Suett stamp, a loose and shambling gait, a slippery tongue, this last the ready midwife to a without-pain-delivered jest; in words, light as air, venting truths deep as the centre; with idlest rhymes tagging conceit when busiest, singing with Lear in the tempest, or Sir Toby at the buttery-hatch.

Jack Bannister[30] and he had the fortune to be more of personal favourites with the town than any actors before or after. The difference, I take it, was this: – Jack was more *beloved* for his sweet, good-natured, moral pretensions. Dicky was more *liked* for his sweet, good-natured, no pretensions at all. Your whole conscience stirred with Bannister's performance of Walter in the Children in the Wood[31] – but Dicky seemed like a thing, as

Shakspeare says of Love, too young to know what conscience is.[32]
He put us into Vesta's days.[33] Evil fled before him – not as from
Jack, as from an antagonist, – but because it could not touch him,
any more than a cannon-ball a fly. He was delivered from the
burthen of that death; and, when Death came himself, not in
metaphor, to fetch Dicky, it is recorded of him by Robert Palmer,[34]
who kindly watched his exit, that he received the last stroke,
neither varying his accustomed tranquillity, nor tune, with the
simple exclamation, worthy to have been recorded in his epitaph –
O La! O La! Bobby!

The elder Palmer (of stage-treading celebrity) commonly played
Sir Toby in those days; but there is a solidity of wit in the jests of
that half-Falstaff which he did not quite fill out. He was as much
too showy as Moody[35] (who sometimes took the part) was dry and
sottish. In sock or buskin there was an air of swaggering gentility
about Jack Palmer. He was a *gentleman* with a slight infusion of
the footman. His brother Bob (of recenter memory) who was his
shadow in every thing while he lived, and dwindled into less than
a shadow afterwards – was a *gentleman* with a little stronger
infusion of the *latter ingredient;* that was all. It is amazing how a
little of the more or less makes a difference in these things. When
you saw Bobby in the Duke's Servant,* you said, what a pity such
a pretty fellow was only a servant. When you saw Jack figuring
in Captain Absolute, you thought you could trace his promotion
to some lady of quality who fancied the handsome fellow in his
topknot, and had bought him a commission. Therefore Jack in
Dick Amlet was insuperable.[36]

Jack had two voices, – both plausible, hypocritical, and insinuat-
ing; but his secondary or supplemental voice still more decisively
histrionic than his common one. It was reserved for the spectator;
and the dramatis personae were supposed to know nothing at all
about it. The *lies* of young Wilding, and the *sentiments* in Joseph
Surface,[37] were thus marked out in a sort of italics to the audience.
This secret correspondence with the company before the curtain
(which is the bane and death of tragedy) has an extremely happy
effect in some kinds of comedy, in the more highly artificial comedy
of Congreve or of Sheridan especially, where the absolute sense of
reality (so indispensable to scenes of interest) is not required, or
would rather interfere to diminish your pleasure. The fact is, you

*High Life Below Stairs. [Lamb's note. The play is by Garrick]

do not believe in such characters as Surface – the villain of
artificial comedy – even while you read or see them. If you did, they
would shock and not divert you. When Ben, in Love for Love,
returns from sea, the following exquisite dialogue occurs at his first
meeting with his father—

> *Sir Sampson.* Thou hast been many a weary league,
> Ben, since I saw thee.
> *Ben.* Ey, ey, been! Been far enough, an that be all. –
> Well, father, and how do all at home? how does brother
> Dick, and brother Val?
> *Sir Sampson.* Dick! body o' me, Dick has been dead
> these two years. I writ you word when you were at
> Leghorn.
> *Ben.* Mess, that's true; Marry, I had forgot. Dick's
> dead, as you say – Well, and how? – I have a many
> questions to ask you—[38]

Here is an instance of insensibility which in real life would be
revolting, or rather in real life could not have co-existed with the
warm-hearted temperament of the character. But when you read
it in the spirit with which such playful selections and specious
combinations rather than strict *metaphrases* of nature should be
taken, or when you saw Bannister play it, it neither did, nor does
wound the moral sense at all. For what is Ben – the pleasant sailor
which Bannister gives us – but a piece of satire – a creation of
Congreve's fancy – a dreamy combination of all the accidents of a
sailor's character – his contempt of money – his credulity to women
– with that necessary estrangement from home which it is just
within the verge of credibility to suppose *might* produce such an
hallucination as is here described. We never think the worse of Ben
for it, or feel it as a stain upon his character. But when an actor
comes, and instead of the delightful phantom – the creature dear to
half-belief – which Bannister exhibited – displays before our eyes a
downright concretion of a Wapping sailor – a jolly warm-hearted
Jack Tar – and nothing else – when instead of investing it with a
delicious confusedness of the head, and a veering undirected goodness of purpose – he gives to it a downright daylight understanding
and a full consciousness of its actions; thrusting forward the
sensibilities of the character with a pretence as if it stood upon
nothing else, and was to be judged by them alone – we feel the

discord of the thing; the scene is disturbed; a real man has got in among the dramatis personae, and puts them out. We want the sailor turned out. We feel that his true place is not behind the curtain but in the first or second gallery.

('On Some of the Old Actors', *Elia*, 1823)

As long as I can remember the play of the Tempest, one passage in it has always set me upon wondering. It has puzzled me beyond measure. In vain I strove to find the meaning of it. I seemed doomed to cherish infinite hopeless curiosity.

It is where Prospero, relating the banishment of Sycorax from Argier, adds—

> – For one thing that she did
> They would not take her life—[39]

how have I pondered over this, when a boy! how have I longed for some authentic memoir of the witch to clear up the obscurity! – Was the story extant in the Chronicles of Algiers? Could I get at it by some fortunate introduction to the Algerine ambassador? Was a voyage thither practicable? The Spectator (I knew) went to Grand Cairo, only to measure a pyramid.[40] Was not the object of my quest of at least as much importance? – The blue-eyed hag – could *she* have done any thing good or meritorious? might that Succubus relent? then might there be hope for the devil. I have often admired since, that none of the commentators have boggled at this passage – how they could swallow this camel – such a tantalising piece of obscurity, such an abortion of an anecdote.

At length, I think I have lighted upon a clue, which may lead to show what was passing in the mind of Shakspeare when he dropped this imperfect rumour. In the 'accurate description of Africa, by John Ogilby (Foiio), 1670,'[41] page 230, I find written, as follows. The marginal title to the narrative is—

Charles the Fifth besieges Algier

In the last place, we will briefly give an Account of the Emperour *Charles* the Fifth, when he besieg'd this city; and of the great Loss he suffer'd therein.

This Prince in the Year One thousand five hundred forty one, having Embarqued upon the Sea an Army of Twenty two thousand Men aboard Eighteen Gallies, and an hundred tall

Ships, not counting the Barques and Shallops, and other small Boats, in which he had engaged the principal of the *Spanish* and *Italian* Nobility, with a good number of the Knights of *Maltha*; he was to Land on the Coast of *Barbary*, at a Cape call'd *Matifou*. From this place unto the City of *Algier* a flat Shore or Strand extends it self for about four Leagues, the which is exceeding favourable to Gallies. There he put ashore with his Army, and in a few days caused a Fortress to be built, which unto this day is call'd *The Castle of the Emperor*.

In the mean time, the City of *Algier* took the Alarm, having in it at that time but Eight hundred *Turks*, and Six thousand *Moors*, poor-spirited men, and unexercised in Martial affairs; besides it was at that time Fortifi'd onely with Walls, and had no Out-works: Insomuch that by reason of its weakness, and the great Forces of the Emperour, it could not in appearance escape taking. In fine, it was Attaqued with such Order, that the Army came up to the very Gates, where the *Chevalier de Sauignac*, a *Frenchman* by Nation, made himself remarkable above all the rest, by the miracles of his Valour. For having repulsed the *Turks*, who having made a Sally at the Gate call'd *Babason*, and there desiring to enter along with them, when he saw that they shut the Gate upon him, he ran his Ponyard into the same, and left it sticking deep therein. They next fell to Battering the City by the Force of Cannon; which the Assailants so weakened, that in that great extremity the Defendants lost their courage, and resolved to surrender.

But as they were thus intending, there was a Witch of the Town, whom the History doth not name, which went to seek out *Assam Aga*, that Commanded within, and pray'd him to make it good yet nine Days longer, with assurance, that within that time he should infallibly see *Algier* delivered from that Siege, and the whole Army of the Enemy dispersed, so that Christians should be as cheap as Birds. In a word, the thing did happen in the manner as foretold; for upon the Twenty first day of *October* in the same Year, there fell a continual Rain upon the land, and so furious a Storm at Sea, that one might have seen Ships hoisted into the Clouds, and in one instant again precipitated into the bottom of the Water: insomuch that that same dreadful Tempest was followed with the loss of fifteen Gallies, and above an hundred other Vessels; which was the cause why the Emperour, seeing his Army wasted by the bad Weather, pursued by a Famine, occasioned by wrack of his Ships, in which was the greatest part of his Victuals and Ammunition, he was constrain'd to raise the Siege, and set Sail for *Sicily*, whither he Retreated with the miserable Reliques of his Fleet.

In the mean time that Witch being acknowledged the Deliverer of *Algier*, was richly remunerated, and the Credit of her Charms authorized. So that ever since Witchcraft hath been very freely tolerated; of which the Chief of the Town, and even those who are esteem'd to be of greatest Sanctity among them, such as are the Marabou's, a Religious Order of their Sect, do for the most part make Profession of it, under a goodly Pretext of certain Revelations which they say they have had from their Prophet *Mahomet*.

And hereupon those of *Algier,* to palliate the shame and the reproaches that are thrown upon them for making use of a Witch in the danger of this Siege, do say, that the loss of the Forces of *Charles* V., was caused by a Prayer of one of their *Marabou's*, named *Cidy Utica*, which was at that time in great Credit, not under the notion of a *Magitian*, but for a person of a holy life. Afterwards in remembrance of their success, they have erected unto him a small mosque without the *Babason* Gate, where he is buried, and in which they keep sundry Lamps burning in honour of him: nay they sometimes repair thither to make their *Sala*, for a testimony of greater Veneration.

Can it be doubted for a moment, that the dramatist had come fresh from reading some *older narrative* of this deliverance of Algier by a witch, and transferred the merit of the deed to his Sycorax, exchanging only the 'rich remuneration,' which did not suit his purpose, to the simple pardon of her life? Ogilby wrote in 1670; but the authorities to which he refers for his Account of Barbary are – Johannes de Leo, or Africanus – Louis Marmol – Diego de Haedo – Johannes Gramaye – Braeves – Cel. Curio – and Diego de Torres[42] – names totally unknown to me – and to which I beg leave to refer the curious reader for his fuller satisfaction.

'Nugae Criticae,' *London Magazine*, November, 1823

The singularity of my case[43] has often led me to enquire into the reasons of the general levity with which the subject of hanging is treated as a topic in this country. I say as a topic: for let the very persons who speak so lightly of the thing at a distance be brought to view the real scene, – let the platform be bona fide exhibited, and the trembling culprit brought forth, – the case is changed; but as a topic of conversation, I appeal to the vulgar jokes which pass current in every street. But why mention them, when the politest authors have agreed in making use of this subject as a source of the ridiculous? Swift, and Pope, and Prior, are fond of recurring to it. Gay has built an entire drama upon this single foundation. The whole interest of the *Beggar's Opera* may be said to hang upon it ... But what shall we say to Shakspeare, who, (not to mention the solution which the *Gravedigger* in *Hamlet* gives of his fellow workman's problem),[44] in that scene in *Measure for Measure*,[45] where the *Clown* calls upon *Master Barnadine* to get up and be hanged, which he declines on the score of being sleepy, has actually gone out of his way to gratify this amiable propensity in his countrymen; for it is plain, from the use that was to be made of his head, and from *Abhorson's* asking, 'Is the axe upon the block, sirrah?' that beheading, and not hanging, was the punishment to which Barnadine was destined. But Shakspeare knew that the axe and the block were pregnant with no ludicrous images, and therefore falsified the historic truth of his own drama (if I may so speak) rather than he would leave out such excellent matter for a jest as the suspending of a fellow-creature in mid air has been ever esteemed to be by Englishmen.

(from 'On the Inconveniences Resulting from being Hanged', *The Reflector*, 1811.)

IV General

In 'An Autobiographical Sketch', Lamb claimed that he 'was the first to draw the Public attention to the old English Dramatists in a work called "Specimens of English Dramatic Writers who lived about the time of Shakspeare".'[1] Although he was by no means the sole pioneer in the field of Elizabethan drama, Lamb must be credited with making excerpts from the plays both readily available and popular. Issued in 1808, the book of selections and notes was among Lamb's earliest publications; he later included a selection of the notes in the 1818 volume of his 'Works'.

Coleridge commented that Lamb's notes are 'full of just and original criticism, expressed with all the freshness of originality.' ('Biographia Literaria', ch. XVIII). Although the notes have been superseded by a wealth of scholarship, they are still valuable in offering pointers to directions in which further studies of Shakespeare's contemporaries might go.

When I selected for publication, in 1808, Specimens of English Dramatic Poets who lived about the time of Shakspeare, the kind of extracts which I was anxious to give were, not so much passages of wit and humour, though the old plays are rich in such, as scenes of passion, sometimes of the deepest quality, interesting situations, serious descriptions, that which is more nearly allied to poetry than to wit, and to tragic rather than to comic poetry. The plays which I made choice of were, with few exceptions, such as treat of human life and manners, rather than masques and Arcadian pastorals, with their train of abstractions, unimpassioned deities, passionate mortals – Claius, and Medorus, and Amintas, and Amarillis. My leading design was, to illustrate what may be called the moral sense of our ancestors. To shew in what manner they felt, when they placed themselves by the power of imagination in trying circumstances, in the conflicts of duty and passion, or the strife of contending duties; what sort of loves and enmities theirs were; how their griefs were tempered, and their full-swoln joys abated: how much of Shakspeare shines in the great men his contemporaries, and how far in his divine mind and manners he surpassed them and

66

all mankind. I was also desirous to bring together some of the most admired scenes of Fletcher and Massinger, in the estimation of the world the only dramatic poets of that age entitled to be considered after Shakspeare, and, by exhibiting them in the same volume with the more impressive scenes of old Marlowe, Heywood, Tourneur, Webster, Ford, and others, to shew what we had slighted, while beyond all proportion we had been crying up one or two favourite names. From the desultory criticisms which accompanied that publication, I have selected a few which I thought would best stand by themselves, as requiring least immediate reference to the play or passage by which they were suggested.

CHRISTOPHER MARLOWE

Lust's Dominion, or the Lascivious Queen.[2] – This tragedy is in King Cambyses' vein;[3] rape, and murder, and superlatives; 'huffing braggart puft lines,'[4] such as the play-writers anterior to Shakspeare are full of, and Pistol but coldly imitates.[5]

Tamburlaine the Great, or the Scythian Shepherd. – The lunes of Tamburlaine are perfect midsummer madness. Nebuchadnazar's are mere modest pretensions compared with the thundering vaunts of this Scythian Shepherd. He comes in, drawn by conquered kings, and reproaches these *pampered jades of Asia* that they can *draw but twenty miles a day.* Till I saw this passage with my own eyes, I never believed that it was any thing more than a pleasant burlesque of mine ancient's.[6] But I can assure my readers that it is soberly set down in a play, which their ancestors took to be serious.

Edward the Second. – In a very different style from mighty Tamburlaine is the tragedy of Edward the Second. The reluctant pangs of abdicating royalty in Edward furnished hints, which Shakspeare scarcely improved in his Richard the Second; and the death-scene of Marlowe's king moves pity and terror beyond any scene antient or modern with which I am acquainted.

The Rich Jew of Malta. – Marlowe's Jew does not approach so near to Shakspeare's, as his Edward the Second does to Richard the Second.[7] Barabas is a mere monster brought in with a large painted nose to please the rabble. He kills in sport, poisons whole nunneries, invents infernal machines. He is just such an exhibition as a century or two earlier might have been played before the Londoners 'by the royal command,' when a general pillage and massacre of the Hebrews had been previously resolved on in the cabinet. It is curious to see a superstition wearing out. The idea of a Jew, which our pious ancestors contemplated with so much horror, has nothing in it now revolting. We have tamed the claws of the beast, and pared its nails, and now we take it to our arms, fondle it, write plays, to flatter it; it is visited by princes, affects a taste, patronizes the arts, and is the only liberal and gentlemanlike thing in Christendom.

Doctor Faustus. – The growing horrors of Faustus's last scene are awfully marked by the hours and half hours as they expire, and bring him nearer and nearer to the exactment of his dire compact. It is indeed an agony and a fearful colluctation.[8] Marlowe is said to have been tainted with atheistical positions, to have denied God and the Trinity. To such a genius the history of Faustus must have been delectable food : to wander in fields where curiosity is forbidden to go, to approach the dark gulf near enough to look in, to be busied in speculations which are the rottenest part of the core of the fruit that fell from the tree of knowledge. Barabas the Jew, and Faustus the conjurer, are offsprings of a mind which at least delighted to dally with interdicted subjects. They both talk a language which a believer would have been tender of putting into the mouth of a character though but in fiction. But the holiest minds have sometimes not thought it reprehensible to counterfeit impiety in the person of another, to bring Vice upon the stage speaking her own dialect; and, themselves being armed with an unction of self-confident impunity, have not scrupled to handle and touch that familiarly, which would be death to others. Milton in the person of Satan has started speculations hardier than any which the feeble armoury of the atheist ever furnished; and the precise, strait-laced Richardson has strengthened Vice, from the mouth of Lovelace, with entangling sophistries and abstruse pleas against her adversary Virtue, which Sedley, Villiers, and Rochester,[9] wanted depth of libertinism enough to have invented.

THOMAS DECKER

Old Fortunatus. – The humour of a frantic lover, in the scene where Orleans to his friend Galloway defends the passion with which himself, being a prisoner in the English king's court, is enamoured to frenzy of the king's daughter Agripyna, is done to the life. Orleans is as passionate an inamorato as any which

Shakspeare ever drew. He is just such another adept in Love's reasons. The sober people of the world are with him

— A swarm of fools
Crowding together to be counted wise. [III. i. 43-44]

He talks 'pure Biron[10] and Romeo,' he is almost as poetical as they, quite as philosophical, only a little madder. After all, Love's sectaries are a reason unto themselves. We have gone retrograde to the noble heresy, since the days when Sidney proselyted our nation to this mixed health and disease; the kindliest sympton, yet the most alarming crisis in the ticklish state of youth; the nourisher and the destroyer of hopeful wits; the mother of twin births, wisdom and folly, valour and weakness; the servitude above freedom; the gentle mind's religion; the liberal superstition.

The Honest Whore – There is in the second part of this play, where Bellafront, a reclaimed harlot, recounts some of the miseries of her profession, a simple picture of honour and shame, contrasted without violence, and expressed without immodesty, which is worth all the *strong lines* against the harlot's profession, with which both parts of this play are offensively crowded. A satirist is always to be suspected, who, to make vice odious, dwells upon all its acts and minutest circumstances with a sort of relish and retrospective fondness. But so near are the boundaries of panegyric and invective, that a worn-out sinner is sometimes found to make the best declaimer against sin. The same high-seasoned descriptions, which in his unregenerate state served but to inflame his appetites, in his new province of a moralist will serve him, a little turned, to expose the enormity of those appetites in other men. When Cervantes with such proficiency of fondness dwells upon the Don's library, who sees not that he has been a great reader of books of knight-errantry – perhaps was at some time of his life in danger of falling into those very extravagancies which he ridiculed so happily in his hero?

JOHN MARSTON

Antonio and Mellida. – The situation of Andrugio and Lucio, in the first part of this tragedy, where Andrugio Duke of Genoa banished his country, with the loss of a son supposed drowned, is cast upon the territory of his mortal enemy the Duke of Venice, with no attendants but Lucio an old nobleman, and a page – resembles that of Lear and Kent in that king's distresses. Andrugio, like Lear, manifests a kinglike impatience, a turbulent greatness, an affected resignation. The enemies which he enters lists to combat, 'Despair and mighty Grief and sharp Impatience,' and the forces which he brings to vanquish them, 'cornets of horse,' &c. are in the boldest style of allegory. They are such a 'race of mourners' as the 'infection of sorrows loud' in the intellect might beget on some 'pregnant cloud' in the imagination.[11] The prologue to the second part, for its passionate earnestness, and for the tragic note of preparation which it sounds, might have preceded one of those old tales of Thebes or Pelops' line, which Milton has so highly commended, as free from the common error of the poets in his day, of 'intermixing comic stuff with tragic sadness and gravity, brought in without discretion corruptly to gratify the people.'[12] It is as solemn a preparative as the 'warning voice which he who saw the Apocalyps heard cry.'[13]

What you Will – O I shall ne'er forget how he went cloath'd. Act I. Scene 1[14] – To judge of the liberality of these notions of dress, we must advert to the days of Gresham,[15] and the consternation which a phenomenon habited like the merchant here described would have excited among the flat round caps and cloth stockings upon 'Change, when those 'original arguments or tokens of a citizen's vocation were in fashion, not more for thrift and usefulness than for distinction and grace.' The blank uniformity to which all professional distinctions in apparel have been long hastening, is one instance of the decay of symbols among us, which, whether it has contributed or not to make us a more intellectual, has certainly made us a less imaginative people. Shakspeare knew the force of signs: a 'malignant and a turban'd Turk.'[16] This 'meal-cap miller,' says the author of God's Revenge against Murder,[17] to express his indignation at an atrocious outrage committed by the miller Pierot upon the person of the fair Marieta.

AUTHOR UNKNOWN

The Merry Devil of Edmonton. – The scene in this delightful comedy, in which Jerningham, 'with the true feeling of a zealous friend,' touches the griefs of Mounchensey,[18] seems written to make the reader happy. Few of our dramatists or novelists have attended enough to this. They torture and wound us abundantly. They are economists only in delight. Nothing can be finer, more gentlemanlike, and nobler, than the conversation and compliments of these young men. How delicious is Raymond Mounchensey's forgetting, in his fears, that Jerningham has a 'Saint in Essex;' and how sweetly his friend reminds him! I wish it could be ascertained, which there is some grounds for believing, that Michael Drayton was the author of this piece. It would add a worthy appendage to the renown of that Panegyrist of my native Earth; who has gone over her soil, in his Polyolbion, with the fidelity of a herald, and the painful love of a son; who has not left a rivulet, so narrow that it may be stept over, without honorable mention; and has animated hills and streams with life and passion beyond the dreams of old mythology.

THOMAS HEYWOOD

A Woman Killed with Kindness. – Heywood is a sort of *prose* Shakspeare. His scenes are to the full as natural and affecting. But we miss *the poet*, that which in Shakspeare always appears out and above the surface of *the nature*. Heywood's characters in this play, for instance, his country gentlemen, &c. are exactly what we see, but of the best kind of what we see, in life. Shakspeare makes us believe, while we are among his lovely creations, that they are nothing but what we are familiar with, as in dreams new things seem old; but we awake, and sigh for the difference.

The English Traveller. – Heywood's preface to this play is interesting, as it shews the heroic indifference about the opinion of posterity, which some of these great writers seem to have felt. There is magnanimity in authorship as in every thing else. His ambition seems to have been confined to the pleasure of hearing the players speak his lines while he lived. It does not appear that he ever contemplated the possibility of being read by after ages. What a slender pittance of fame was motive sufficient to the production of such plays as the English Traveller, the Challenge for Beauty, and the Woman Killed with Kindness! Posterity is bound to take care that a writer loses nothing by such a noble modesty.

THOMAS MIDDLETON

The Witch. – Though some resemblance may be traced between the charms in Macbeth, and the incantations in this play, which is supposed to have preceded it, this coincidence will not detract much

71

from the originality of Shakspeare. His witches are distinguished from the witches of Middleton by essential differences. These are creatures to whom man or woman, plotting some dire mischief, might resort for occasional consultation. Those originate deeds of blood, and begin bad impulses to men. From the moment that their eyes first meet with Macbeth's, he is spell-bound. That meeting sways his destiny. He can never break the fascination. These witches can hurt the body, those have power over the soul. Hecate in Middleton has a son, a low buffoon: the hags of Shakspeare have neither child of their own, nor seem to be descended from any parent. They are foul anomalies, of whom we know not whence they are sprung, nor whether they have beginning or ending. As they are without human passions, so they seem to be without human relations. They come with thunder and lightning, and vanish to airy music. This is all we know of them. Except Hecate, they have no *names*; which heightens their mysteriousness. The names, and some of the properties, which the other author has given to his hags, excite smiles. The Weird Sisters are serious things. Their presence cannot co-exist with mirth. But, in a lesser degree, the witches of Middleton are fine creations. Their power too is, in some measure, over the mind. They raise jars, jealousies, strifes, 'like a thick scurf' over life.

WILLIAM ROWLEY, – THOMAS DECKER, – JOHN FORD, &c.

The Witch of Edmonton. – Mother Sawyer, in this wild play, differs from the hags of both Middleton and Shakspeare. She is the plain traditional old woman witch of our ancestors; poor, deformed, and ignorant; the terror of villages, herself amenable to a justice. That should be a hardy sheriff, with the power of the county at his heels, that would lay hands upon the Weird Sisters. They are of another jurisdiction. But upon the common and received opinion, the author (or authors) have engrafted strong fancy. There is something frightfully earnest in her invocations to the Familiar.

CYRIL TOURNEUR

The Revenger's Tragedy. – The reality and life of the dialogue, in which Vindici and Hippolito first tempt their mother, and then threaten her with death for consenting to the dishonour of their sister, passes any scenical illusion I ever felt. I never read it but my ears tingle, and I feel a hot blush overspread my cheeks, as if I were presently about to proclaim such malefactions of myself as the brothers here rebuke in their unnatural parent, in words more keen and dagger-like than those which Hamlet speaks to his mother.[19] Such power has the passion of shame truly personated, not only to strike guilty creatures unto the soul, but to 'appal' even those that are 'free.'

JOHN WEBSTER

The Duchess of Malfy. – All the several parts of the dreadful apparatus with which the death of the Duchess is ushered in, the waxen images which counterfeit death, the wild masque of madmen, the tomb-maker, the bellman, the living person's dirge, the mortification by degrees, – are not more remote from the conceptions of ordinary vengeance, than the strange character of suffering which they seem to bring upon their victim is out of the imagination of ordinary poets. As they are not like inflictions of this life, so her language seems not of this world. She has lived among horrors till she is become 'native and endowed [indued] unto that element.' She speaks the dialect of despair; her tongue has a smatch of Tartarus and the souls in bale. To move a horror skilfully, to touch a soul to the quick, to lay upon fear as much as it can bear, to wean and weary a life till it is ready to drop, and then step in with mortal instruments to take its last forfeit: this only a Webster can do. Inferior geniuses may 'upon horror's head horrors accumulate,' but they cannot do this. They mistake quantity for quality; they 'terrify babes with painted devils;' but they know not how a soul is to be moved.[20] Their terrors want dignity, their affrightments are without decorum.

The White Devil, or Vittoria Corombona. – This White Devil of Italy sets off a bad cause so speciously, and pleads with such an innocence-resembling boldness, that we seem to see that matchless beauty of her face which inspires such gay confidence into her, and are ready to expect, when she has done her pleadings, that her very judges, her accusers, the grave ambassadors who sit as spectators, and all the court, will rise and make proffer to defend her in spite of the utmost conviction of her guilt; as the Shepherds in Don Quixote make proffer to follow the beautiful Shepherdess Marcela, 'without making any profit of her manifest resolution made there in their hearing.'[21]

> So sweet and lovely does she make the shame,
> Which, like a canker in the fragrant rose,
> Does spot the beauty of her budding name! [22]

I never saw any thing like the funeral dirge in this play, for the death of Marcello, except the ditty which reminds Ferdinand of his drowned father in the Tempest.[23] As that is of the water, watery; so this is of the earth, earthy. Both have that intenseness of feeling, which seems to resolve itself into the element which it contemplates.

In a note on the Spanish Tragedy in the Specimens, I have said that there is nothing in the undoubted plays of Jonson which would authorize us to suppose that he could have supplied the additions to Hieronymo. I suspected the agency of some more potent spirit. I thought that Webster might have furnished them. They seemed full of that wild, solemn, preternatural cast of grief which bewilders us in the Duchess of Malfy. On second consideration, I think this a hasty criticism. They are more like the overflowing griefs and talking distraction of Titus Andronicus. The sorrows of the Duchess set inward; if she talks, it is little more than soliloquy imitating conversation in a kind of bravery.

FULKE GREVILLE, LORD BROOKE

Alaham, Mustapha. – The two tragedies of Lord Brooke, printed among his poems, might with more propriety have been termed political treatises than plays. Their author has strangely contrived to make passion, character, and interest, of the highest order, subservient to the expression of state dogmas and mysteries. He is nine parts Machiavel and Tacitus, for one part Sophocles or Seneca. In this writer's estimate of the powers of the mind, the understanding must have held a most tyrannical pre-eminence. Whether we look into his plays, or his most passionate love-poems, we shall find all frozen and made rigid with intellect. The finest movements of the human heart, the utmost grandeur of which the soul is capable, are essentially comprised in the actions and speeches of Caelica and Camena. Shakspeare, who seems to have had a pecular delight in contemplating womanly perfection, whom for his many sweet images of female excellence all women are in an especial manner bound to love, has not raised the ideal of the female character higher than Lord Brooke, in these two women, has done. But it requires a study equivalent to the learning of a new language to understand their meaning when they speak. It is indeed hard to hit:

> Much like thy riddle, Samson, in one day
> Or seven though one should musing sit.[24]

It is as if a being of pure intellect should take upon him to express the emotions of our sensitive natures. There would be all knowledge, but sympathetic expressions would be wanting.

GEORGE CHAPMAN

Bussy D'Ambois, Byron's Conspiracy, Byron's Tragedy, &c. &c – Webster has happily characterised the 'full and heightened style' of Chapman, who, of all the English play-writers, perhaps approaches nearest to Shakspeare in the descriptive and didactic, in passages which are less purely dramatic. He could not go out of himself, as Shakspeare could shift at pleasure, to inform and animate other existences, but in himself he had an eye to perceive and a soul to embrace all forms and modes of being. He would have made a great epic poet, if indeed he has not abundantly shewn himself to be one; for his Homer is not so properly a translation as the stories of Achilles and Ulysses re-written. The earnestness and passion which he has put into every part of these poems, would be incredible to a reader of mere modern translations. His almost Greek zeal for the glory of his heroes can only be paralleled by that fierce spirit of Hebrew bigotry, with which Milton, as if personating one of the zealots of the old law, clothed himself when he sat down to paint the acts of Samson against the uncircumcised. The great obstacle to Chapman's translations being read, is their unconquerable quaintness. He pours out in the same breath the most just and natural, and the most violent and crude expressions. He seems to grasp at whatever words come first to hand while the enthusiasm is upon him, as if all other must be inadequate to the divine meaning. But passion (the all in all in poetry) is every where present, raising the low, dignifying the mean, and putting sense into the absurd. He makes his readers glow, weep, tremble, take any affection which he pleases, be moved by words, or in spite of them, be disgusted and overcome their disgust.

75

FRANCIS BEAUMONT. – JOHN FLETCHER

Maid's Tragedy. – One characteristic of the excellent old poets is, their being able to bestow grace upon subjects which naturally do not seem susceptible of any. I will mention two instances. Zelmane in the Arcadia of Sidney,[25] and Helena in the All's Well that Ends Well of Shakspeare. What can be more unpromising at first sight, than the idea of a young man disguising himself in woman's attire, and passing himself off for a woman among women; and that for a long space of time? Yet Sir Philip has preserved so matchless a decorum, that neither does Pryocles' manhood suffer any stain for the effeminacy of Zelmane, nor is the respect due to the princesses at all diminished when the deception comes to be known. In the sweetly constituted mind of Sir Philip Sidney, it seems as if no ugly. thought or unhandsome meditation could find a harbour. He turned all that he touched into images of honour and virtue. Helena in Shakspeare is a young woman seeking a man in marriage. The ordinary rules of courtship are reversed, the habitual feelings are crossed. Yet with such exquisite address this dangerous subject is handled, that Helena's forwardness loses her no honour; delicacy dispenses with its laws in her favour, and nature, in her single case, seems content to suffer a sweet violation. Aspatia, in the Maid's Tragedy, is a character equally difficult, with Helena, of being managed with grace. She too is a slighted woman, refused by the man who had once engaged to marry her. Yet it is artfully contrived, that while we pity we respect her, and she descends without degradation. Such wonders true poetry and passion can do, to confer dignity upon subjects which do not seem capable of it. But Aspatia must not be compared at all points with Helena; she does not so absolutely predominate over her situation but she suffers some diminution, some abatement of the full lustre of the female character, which Helena never does. Her character has many degrees of sweetness, some of delicacy; but it has weakness, which, if we do not despise, we are sorry for. After all, Beaumont and Fletcher were but an inferior sort of Shakspeares and Sidneys.

Philaster. – The character of Bellario must have been extremely popular in its day. For many years after the date of Philaster's first exhibition on the stage, scarce a play can be found without one of these women pages in it, following in the train of some preengaged lover, calling on the gods to bless her happy rival (his mistress), whom no doubt she secretly curses in her heart, giving rise to many pretty *equivoques* by the way on the confusion of sex, and either made happy at last by some surprising turn of fate, or dismissed with the joint pity of the lovers and the audience. Donne has a copy of verses to his mistress, dissuading her from a resolution which she seems to have taken up from some of these scenical representations, of following him abroad as a page.[26] It is so earnest, so weighty, so rich in poetry, in sense, in wit, and pathos, that it deserves to be read as a solemn close in future to all such sickly fancies as he there deprecates.

JOHN FLETCHER

Thierry and Theodoret. – The scene where Ordella offers her life a sacrifice, that the king of France may not be childless, I have always considered as the finest in all Fletcher, and Ordella to be the most perfect notion of the female heroic character, next to Calantha in the Broken Heart. She is a piece of sainted nature. Yet noble as the whole passage is, it must be confessed that the manner of it, compared with Shakspeare's finest scenes, is faint and languid. Its motion is circular, not progressive. Each line revolves on itself in a sort of separate orbit. They do not join into one another like a running-hand. Fletcher's ideas moved slow; his versification, though sweet, is tedious, it stops at every turn; he lays line upon line, making up one after the other, adding image to image so deliberately, that we see their junctures. Shakspeare mingles every thing, runs line into line, embarrasses sentences and metaphors; before one idea has burst its shell, another is hatched and clamorous for disclosure. Another striking difference between Fletcher and Shakspeare, is the fondness of the former for unnatural and violent situations. He seems to have thought that nothing great could be produced in an ordinary way. The chief incidents in some of his most admired tragedies shew this.** Shakspeare had nothing of this contortion in his mind, none of that craving after violent situations, and flights of strained and improbable virtue, which I think always betrays an imperfect moral sensibility. The wit of Fletcher is excellent* like his serious scenes, but there is something strained and far-fetched

**Wife for a Month, Cupid's Revenge, Double Marriage, &c. [Lamb's note]
*Wit without Money, and his comedies generally. [Lamb's note]

77

Charles Lamb on Shakespeare

in both. He is too mistrustful of Nature, he always goes a little on one side of her. Shakspeare chose her without a reserve: and had riches, power, understanding, and length of days, with her, for a dowry.

Faithful Shepherdess. – If all the parts of this delightful pastoral had been in unison with its many innocent scenes and sweet lyric intermixtures, it had been a poem fit to vie with Comus or the Arcadia, to have been put into the hands of boys and virgins, to have made matter for young dreams, like the loves of Hermia and Lysander.[27] But a spot is on the face of this Diana.[28] Nothing short of infatuation could have driven Fletcher upon mixing with this 'blessedness' such an ugly deformity as Cloe, the wanton shepherdess! If Cloe was meant to set off Clorin by contrast, Fletcher should have known that such weeds by juxta-position do not set off, but kill sweet flowers.

PHILIP MASSINGER. – THOMAS DECKER

The Virgin Martyr. – This play has some beauties of so very high an order, that with all my respect for Massinger, I do not think he had poetical enthusiasm capable of rising up to them. His associate Decker, who wrote Old Fortunatus, had poetry enough for any thing. The very impurities which obtrude themselves among the sweet pieties of this play, like Satan among the Sons of Heaven, have a strength of contrast, a raciness, and a glow in them, which are beyond Massinger. They are to the religion of the rest what Caliban is to Miranda.

JAMES SHIRLEY

Claims a place amongst the worthies of this period, not so much for any transcendent talent in himself, as that he was the last of a great race, all of whom spoke nearly the same language, and had a set of moral feelings and notions in common. A new language, and quite a new turn of tragic and comic interest, came in with the Restoration.

From *Characters of Dramatic Writers Contemporary With Shakspeare*, 1818

78

To your enquiry respecting a selection from Bp. Taylor[29] I answer – it cannot be done, and if it could, it would not *take* with John Bull.[30] – It cannot be done, for who can disentangle and unthread the rich texture of Nature and Poetry sewn so thick into a stout coat of theology, without spoiling both *lace* and *coat*? how beggarly and how bald do even Shakspeare's Princely Pieces look, when thus violently divorced from *connexion* and *circumstance*! When we meet with To be or not to be – or Jacques's moralizings upon the Deer – or Brutus and Cassius' quarrel and reconciliation – in an Enfield Speaker, or in Elegant Extracts[31] – how we stare and will scarcely acknowledge to ourselves (what we are conscious we feel) that they are flat and have no power. Something exactly like this have I experienced when I have picked out similes and stars from Holy Dying and shewn them per se, as you'd shew specimens of minerals or pieces of rock. Compare the grand effect of the Star-paved firmament – and imagine a boy capable of picking out those pretty twinklers one by one and playing at chuck-farthing with them. – Every thing in heaven and earth, in man and in story, in books and in fancy, acts by Confederacy, by juxtaposition, by circumstance and place. – Consider a fine family – (if I were not writing to you I might instance your own) of sons and daughters with a respectable father and a handsome mother at their head, all met in one house, and happy round one table. – Earth cannot show a more lovely and venerable sight, such as the Angels in heaven might lament that in their country there is no marrying or giving in marriage. Take and split this Body into individuals – show the separate caprices, vagaries, etc., of Charles, Rob, or Plum, one a quaker, another a churchman. The eldest daughter seeking a husband out of the pale of parental faith – another warping perhaps – the father a prudent, circumspective, do-me-good sort of a man *blest* with children whom no ordinary rules can circumscribe. – I have not room for all particulars – but just as this happy and venerable Body of a family loses by splitting and considering individuals too nicely, so it is when we pick out Best Bits out of a great writer. 'Tis the *Sum* total of his mind which *affects* us.

From a Letter to Robert Lloyd, 18 November, 1801.

I have Ray's *Collections of English Words not generally Used*, 1691; and in page 60 ('North Country words') occurs *'Rynt ye'* – 'by your leave,' 'stands handsomely.' As, 'Rynt you, witch,' quoth Besse Locket to her mother; Proverb, Cheshire. – Doubtless this is the 'Aroint' of Shakspeare.

In the same collection I find several Shaksperisms. 'Rooky' wood: [32] a Northern word for 'reeky', 'misty' etc. 'Shandy' a north country word for 'wild'. Sterne was York.

From a letter to William Hone, 19 May, 1823.

V   Tales from Shakespear

In 1806, Mary Lamb was asked by William Godwin and his wife to prepare a children's book of stories from Shakespeare's plays. Charles Lamb, perhaps because of the nervous strain the task might impose on his sister, undertook to write the tragic stories. In a letter to Wordsworth of 29 January, 1807, he noted: 'I am answerable for Lear, Macbeth, Timon, Romeo, Hamlet, Othello, for occasionally a tail piece or correction of grammar, for none of the cuts and all of the spelling. The rest is my Sister's. – We think Pericles of hers the best, and Othello of mine – but I hope all have some good.'

The book was published, under Charles Lamb's name, in 1807 and has run into scores of editions, including many translations into foreign languages.

KING LEAR

Lear, king of Britain, had three daughters; Gonerill, wife to the duke of Albany; Regan, wife to the duke of Cornwall; and Cordelia, a young maid, for whose love the king of France and duke of Burgundy were joint suitors, and were at this time making stay for that purpose in the court of Lear.

The old king, worn out with age and the fatigues of government, he being more than fourscore years old, determined to take no further part in state affairs, but to leave the management to younger strengths, that he might have time to prepare for death, which must at no long period ensue. With this intent he called his three daughters to him, to know from their own lips which of them loved him best, that he might part his kingdom among them in such proportions as their affection for him should seem to deserve.

Gonerill, the eldest, declared that she loved her father more than words could give out, that he was dearer to her than the light of her own eyes, dearer than life and liberty, with a deal of such professing stuff, which is easy to counterfeit where there is no real love, only a few fine words delivered with confidence being wanted in that case. The king, delighted to hear from her own mouth this assurance of her love, and thinking truly that her heart went with it, in a fit of fatherly fondness bestowed upon her and her husband one third of his ample kingdom.

Then calling to him his second daughter, he demanded what she had to say. Regan, who was made of the same hollow metal as her sister, was not a whit behind in her professions, but rather declared that what her sister had spoken came short of the love which she professed to bear for his highness: insomuch that she found all other joys dead, in comparison with the pleasure which she took in the love of her dear king and father.

Lear blest himself in having such loving children, as he thought; and could do no less, after the handsome assurances which Regan had made, than bestow a third of his kingdom upon her and her husband, equal in size to that which he had already given away to Gonerill.

Then turning to his youngest daughter Cordelia, whom he called his joy, he asked what she had to say; thinking no doubt that she would glad his ears with the same loving speeches which her sisters had uttered, or rather that her expressions would be so much stronger than theirs, as she had always been his darling, and favoured by him above either of them. But Cordelia, disgusted with the flattery of her sisters, whose hearts she knew were far from their lips, and seeing that all their coaxing speeches were only intended to wheedle the old king out of his dominions, that they and their husbands might reign in his life-time, made no other reply but this, that she loved his majesty according to her duty, neither more nor less.

The king, shocked with this appearance of ingratitude in his favourite child, desired her to consider her words, and to mend her speech, lest it should mar her fortunes.

Cordelia then told her father, that he was her father, that he had given her breeding, and loved her, that she returned those duties back as was most fit, and did obey him, love him, and most honour him. But that she could not frame her mouth to such large speeches as her sisters had done, or promise to love nothing else in the world. Why had her sisters husbands, if (as they said) they had no love for any thing but their father? If she should ever wed, she was sure the lord to whom she gave her hand would want half her love, half of her care and duty; she should never marry like her sisters, to love her father all.

Cordelia, who in earnest loved her old father, even almost as extravagantly as her sisters pretended to do, would have plainly told him so at any other time, in more daughter-like and loving terms, and without these qualifications which did indeed sound a little ungracious: but after the crafty flattering speeches of her sisters, which she had seen draw such extravagant rewards, she thought the handsomest thing she could do was to love and be silent. This put her affection out of suspicion of mercenary ends, and shewed that she loved, but not for gain; and that her professions, the less ostentatious they were, had so much the more of truth and sincerity than her sisters.

This plainness of speech, which Lear called pride, so enraged the old monarch – who in his best of times always shewed much of spleen and rashness, and in whom the dotage incident to old age had so clouded over his reason, that he could not discern truth from flattery, nor a gay painted speech from words that came from the heart – that in a fury of resentment he retracted the third part of his kingdom which yet remained, and which he had reserved for Cordelia, and gave it away from her, sharing it equally between her two sisters and their husbands, the dukes of Albany and Cornwall: whom he now called to him, and in presence of all his courtiers, bestowing a coronet between them, invested them jointly with all the power, revenue, and execution of government, only retaining to himself the name of king; all the rest of royalty he resigned: with this reservation, that himself, with a hundred knights for his attendants, was to be maintained by monthly course in each of his daughter's palaces in turn.

So preposterous a disposal of his kingdom, so little guided by reason, and so much by passion, filled all his courtiers with astonishment and sorrow; but none of them had the courage to interpose between this incensed king and his wrath, except the earl of Kent, who was beginning to speak a good word for Cordelia, when the passionate Lear on pain of death commanded him to desist: but the good Kent was not so to be repelled. He had been ever loyal to Lear, whom he had honoured as a king, loved as a father, followed as a master: and had never esteemed his life further than as a pawn to wage against his royal master's enemies, nor feared to lose it when Lear's safety was the motive: nor now that Lear was most his own enemy did this faithful servant of the king forget his old principles, but manfully opposed Lear, to do Lear good; and was unmannerly only because Lear was mad. He

Lear and Fool.

had been a most faithful counsellor in times past to the king, and he besought him now, that he would see with his eyes (as he had done in many weighty matters), and go by his advice still; and in his best consideration recall this hideous rashness: for he would answer with his life his judgment, that Lear's youngest daughter did not love him least, nor were those empty-hearted whose low sound gave no token of hollowness. When power bowed to flattery, honour was bound to plainness. For Lear's threats, what could he do to him, whose life was already at his service? that should not hinder duty from speaking.

The honest freedom of this good earl of Kent only stirred up the king's wrath the more, and like a frantic patient who kills his physician, and loves his mortal disease, he banished this true servant, and allotted him but five days to make his preparations for departure; but if on the sixth his hated person was found within the realm of Britain, that moment was to be his death. And Kent bade farewell to the king, and said, that since he chose to shew himself in such fashion, it was but banishment to stay there: and before he went, he recommended Cordelia to the protection of the gods, the maid who had so rightly thought, and so discreetly spoken; and only wished that her sister's large speeches might be answered with deeds of love: and then he went, as he said, to shape his old course to a new country.

The king of France and duke of Burgundy were now called in to hear the determination of Lear about his youngest daughter, and to know whether they would persist in their courtship to Cordelia, now that she was under her father's displeasure, and had no fortune but her own person to recommend her: and the duke of Burgundy declined the match, and would not take her to wife upon such, conditions; but the king of France, understanding what the nature of the fault had been which had lost her the love of her father, that it was only a tardiness of speech, and the not being able to frame her tongue to flattery like her sisters, took this young maid by the hand, and saying that her virtues were a dowry above a kingdom, bade Cordelia to take farewell of her sisters, and of her father, though he had been unkind, and she should go with him, and be queen of him and of fair France, and reign over fairer possessions than her sisters: and he called the duke of Burgundy in contempt a waterish duke, because his love for this young maid had in a moment run all away like water.

Then Cordelia with weeping eyes took leave of her sisters, and besought them to love their father well, and make good their professions: and they sullenly told her not to prescribe to them, for they knew their duty; but to strive to content her husband, who had taken her (as they tauntingly expressed it) as Fortune's alms. And Cordelia with a heavy heart departed, for she knew the cunning of her sisters, and she wished her father in better hands than she was about to leave him in.

Cordelia was no sooner gone, than the devilish dispositions of her sisters began to shew themselves in their true colours. Even before the expiration of the first month which Lear was to spend by agreement with his eldest daughter Gonerill, the old king began to find out the difference between promises and performances. This wretch having got from her father all that he had to bestow, even to the giving away of the crown from off his head, began to grudge even those small remnants of royalty which the old man had reserved to himself, to please his fancy with the idea of being still a king. She could not bear to see him and his hundred knights. Every time she met her father, she put on a frowning countenance; and when the old man wanted to speak with her, she would feign sickness or any thing to be rid of the sight of him; for it was plain that she esteemed his old age a useless burden, and his attendants an unnecessary expense: not only she herself slackened in her expressions of duty to the king, but by her example, and (it is to be feared) not without her private instructions, her very servants affected to treat him with neglect, and would either refuse to obey his orders, or still more contemptuously pretend not to hear them. Lear could not but perceive this alteration in the behaviour of his daughter, but he shut his eyes against it as long as he could, as people commonly are unwilling to believe the unpleasant consequences which their own mistakes and obstinacy have brought upon them.

True love and fidelity are no more to be estranged by *ill*, than falsehood and hollow-heartedness can be conciliated by *good usage*. This eminently appears in the instance of the good earl of Kent, who, though banished by Lear, and his life made forfeit if he were found in Britain, chose to stay and abide all consequences, as long as there was a chance of his being useful to the king his master. See to what mean shifts and disguises poor loyalty is forced to submit sometimes; yet it counts nothing base or unworthy so as

it can but do service where it owes an obligation! In the disguise
of a serving-man, all his greatness and pomp laid aside, this good
earl proffered his services to the king, who not knowing him to be
Kent in that disguise, but pleased with a certain plainness, or rather
bluntness in his answers which the earl put on (so different from
that smooth oily flattery which he had so much reason to be sick of,
having found the effects not answerable in his daughter), a bargain
was quickly struck, and Lear took Kent into his service by the
name of Caius, as he called himself, never suspecting him to be
his once great favourite, the high and mighty earl of Kent.

This Caius quickly found means to shew his fidelity and love to
his royal master: for Gonerill's steward that same day behaving
in a disrespectful manner to Lear, and giving him saucy looks
and language, as no doubt he was secretly encouraged to do by his
mistress, Caius not enduring to hear so open an affront put upon
majesty, made no more ado but presently tript up his heels, and
laid the unmannerly slave in the kennel: for which friendly service
Lear became more and more attached to him.

Nor was Kent the only friend Lear had. In his degree, and as far
as so insignificant a personage could shew his love, the poor fool,
or jester, that had been of his palace while Lear had a palace, as
it was the custom of kings and great personages at that time to keep
a fool (as he was called) to make them sport after serious business: –
this poor fool clung to Lear after he had given away his crown, and
by his witty sayings would keep up his good humour; though he
could not refrain sometimes from jeering at his master for his
imprudence, in uncrowning himself, and giving all away to his
daughters: at which time, as he rhymingly expressed it, these
daughters

> For sudden joy did weep,
>   And he for sorrow sung,
> That such a king should play bo-peep,
>   And go the fools among.

And in such wild sayings, and scraps of songs, of which he had
plenty, this pleasant honest fool poured out his heart even in the
presence of Gonerill herself, in many a bitter taunt and jest which
cut to the quick; such as comparing the king to the hedge-
sparrow, who feeds the young of the cuckoo till they grow old
enough, and then has its head bit off for its pains: and saying, that

an ass may know when the cart draws the horse (meaning that Lear's daughters, that ought to go behind, now ranked before their father); and that Lear was no longer Lear, but the shadow of Lear: for which free speeches he was once or twice threatened to be whipt.

The coolness and falling off of respect which Lear had begun to perceive, were not all which this foolish-fond father was to suffer from his unworthy daughter: she now plainly told him that his staying in her palace was inconvenient so long as he insisted upon keeping up an establishment of a hundred knights; that this establishment was useless and expensive, and only served to fill her court with riot and feasting; and she prayed him that he would lessen their number, and keep none but old men about him, such as himself, and fitting his age.

Lear at first could not believe his eyes or ears, nor that it was his daughter who spoke so unkindly. He could not believe that she who had received a crown from him could seek to cut off his train, and grudge him the respect due to his old age. But she persisting in her undutiful demand, the old man's rage was so excited, that he called her a detested kite, and said that she spoke an untruth: and so indeed she did, for the hundred knights were all men of choice behaviour and sobriety of manners, skilled in all particulars of duty, and not given to rioting or feasting as she said. And he bid his horses to be prepared, for he would go to his other daughter, Regan, he and his hundred knights: and he spoke of ingratitude, and said it was a marble-hearted devil, and shewed more hideous in a child than the sea-monster. And he cursed his eldest daughter Gonerill so as was terrible to hear: praying that she might never have a child, or if she had, that it might live to return that scorn and contempt upon her, which she had shewn to him: that she might feel how sharper than a serpent's tooth it was to have a thankless child. And Gonerill's husband, the duke of Albany, beginning to excuse himself for any share which Lear might suppose he had in the unkindness, Lear would not hear him out, but in a rage ordered his horses to be saddled, and set out with his followers for the abode of Regan, his other daughter. And Lear thought to himself, how small the fault of Cordelia (if it was a fault) now appeared, in comparison with her sister's, and he wept; and then he was ashamed that such a creature as Gonerill should have so much power over his manhood as to make him weep.

Regan and her husband were keeping their court in great pomp and state at their palace: and Lear dispatched his servant Caius with letters to his daughter, that she might be prepared for his reception, while he and his train followed after. But it seems that Gonerill had been beforehand with him, sending letters also to Regan, accusing her father of waywardness and ill humours, and advising her not to receive so great a train as he was bringing with him. This messenger arrived at the same time with Caius, and Caius and he met: and who should it be but Caius' old enemy the steward, whom he had formerly tript up by the heels for his saucy behaviour to Lear. Caius not liking the fellow's look, and suspecting what he came for, began to revile him, and challenged him to fight, which the fellow refusing, Caius, in a fit of honest passion, beat him soundly, as such a mischief-maker and carrier of wicked messages deserved: which coming to the ears of Regan and her husband, they ordered Caius to be put in the stocks, though he was a messenger from the king her father, and in that character demanded the highest respect: so that the first thing the king saw when he entered the castle, was his faithful servant Caius sitting in that disgraceful situation.

This was but a bad omen of the reception which he was to expect; but a worse followed, when upon enquiry for his daughter and her husband, he was told they were weary with travelling all night, and could not see him: and when lastly, upon his insisting in a positive and angry manner to see them, they came to greet him, whom should he see in their company but the hated Gonerill, who had come to tell her own story, and set her sister against the king her father!

This sight much moved the old man, and still more to see Regan take her by the hand: and he asked Gonerill if she was not ashamed to look upon his old white beard? And Regan advised him to go home again with Gonerill, and live with her peaceably, dismissing half of his attendants, and to ask her forgiveness; for he was old and wanted discretion, and must be ruled and led by persons that had more discretion than himself. And Lear shewed how preposterous that would sound, if he were to down on his knees, and beg of his own daughter for food and raiment, and he argued against such an unnatural dependence; declaring his resolution never to return with her, but to stay where he was with Regan, he and his hundred knights: for he said that she had not forgot the half of the kingdom which he had endowed her with, and that her eyes were not fierce like Gonerill's, but mild and kind. And he said that rather than return to Gonerill, with half his train cut off, he would go over to France, and beg a wretched pension of the king there, who had married his youngest daughter without a portion.

But he was mistaken in expecting kinder treatment of Regan than he had experienced from her sister Gonerill. As if willing to outdo her sister in unfilial behaviour, she declared that she thought fifty knights too many to wait upon him: that five-and-twenty were enough. Then Lear, nigh heartbroken, turned to Gonerill, and said that he would go back with her, for her fifty doubled five-and-twenty, and so her love was twice as much as Regan's. But Gonerill excused herself, and said, what need of so many as five-and-twenty? or even ten? or five? when he might be waited upon by her servants, or her sister's servants? So these two wicked daughters, as if they strove to exceed each other in cruelty to their old father who had been so good to them, by little and little would have abated him of all his train, all respect (little enough for him that once commanded a kingdom) which was left him to shew that he had once been a king! Not that a splendid train is essential to happiness, but from a king to a beggar is a hard change, from commanding millions to be without one attendant; and it was the ingratitude in his daughters' denying it, more than what he would suffer by the want of it, which pierced this poor king to the heart: insomuch that with this double ill usage, and vexation for having so foolishly given away a kingdom, his wits began to be unsettled, and while he said he knew not what, he vowed revenge against those unnatural hags, and to make examples of them that should be a terror to the earth!

While he was thus idly threatening what his weak arm could never execute, night came on, and a loud storm of thunder and lightning with rain; and his daughters still persisting in their resolution not to admit his followers, he called for his horses, and chose rather to encounter the utmost fury of the storm abroad, than stay under the same roof with these ungrateful daughters: and they saying that the injuries which wilful men procure to themselves are their just punishment, suffered him to go in that condition, and shut their doors upon him.

The winds were high, and the rain and storm increased, when

the old man sallied forth to combat with the elements, less sharp than his daughters' unkindness. For many miles about there was scarce a bush; and there upon a heath, exposed to the fury of the storm in a dark night, did king Lear wander out, and defy the winds and the thunder: and he bid the winds to blow the earth into the sea, or swell the waves of the sea till they drowned the earth, that no token might remain of any such ungrateful animal as man. The old king was now left with no other companion than the poor fool, who still abided with him, with his merry conceits striving to outjest misfortune, saying, it was but a naughty night to swim in, and truly the king had better go in and ask his daughter's blessing:

> But he that has a little tiny wit,
> With heigh ho, the wind and the rain!
> Must make content with his fortunes fit,
> Though the rain it raineth every day:

and swearing it was a brave night to cool a lady's pride.

Thus poorly accompanied this once great monarch was found by his ever faithful servant the good earl of Kent, now transformed to Caius, who ever followed close at his side, though the king did not know him to be the earl; and he said, 'Alas! sir, are you here? creatures that love night, love not such nights as these. This dreadful storm has driven the beasts to their hiding places. Man's nature cannot endure the affliction or the fear.' And Lear rebuked him and said, these lesser evils were not felt, where a greater malady was fixed. When the mind is at ease, the body has leisure to be delicate; but the tempest in his mind did take all feeling else from his senses, but of that which beat at his heart. And he spoke of filial ingratitude, and said it was all one as if the mouth should tear the hand for lifting food to it; for parents were hands and food and every thing to children.

But the good Caius still persisting in his intreaties that the king would not stay out in the open air, at last persuaded him to enter a little wretched hovel which stood upon the heath, where the fool first entering suddenly ran back terrified, saying that he had seen a spirit. But upon examination this spirit proved to be nothing more than a poor Bedlam-beggar, who had crept into this deserted hovel for shelter, and with his talk about devils frighted the fool, one of those poor lunatics who are either mad, or feign to be so, the better to extort charity from the compassionate country-people;

who go about the country, calling themselves poor Tom and poor Turlygood saying, 'Who gives any thing to poor Tom?' sticking pins and nails and sprigs of rosemary into their arms to make them bleed; and with such horrible actions, partly by prayers, and partly with lunatic curses, they move or terrify the ignorant country-folks into giving them alms. This poor fellow was such a one; and the king seeing him in so wretched a plight, with nothing but a blanket about his loins to cover his nakedness, could not be persuaded but that the fellow was some father who had given all away to his daughters, and brought himself to that pass: for nothing he thought could bring a man to such wretchedness but the having unkind daughters.

And from this and many such wild speeches which he uttered, the good Caius plainly perceived that he was not in his perfect mind, but that his daughters' ill usage had really made him go mad. And now the loyalty of this worthy earl of Kent shewed itself in more essential services than he had hitherto found opportunity to perform. For with the assistance of some of the king's attendants who remained loyal, he had the person of his royal master removed at day-break to the castle of Dover, where his own friends and influence, as earl of Kent, chiefly lay: and himself embarking for France, hastened to the court of Cordelia, and did there in such moving terms represent the pitiful condition of her royal father, and set out in such lively colours the inhumanity of her sisters, that this good and loving child with many tears besought the king her husband, that he would give her leave to embark for England with a sufficient power to subdue these cruel daughters and their husbands, and restore the old king her father to his throne; which being granted, she set forth, and with a royal army landed at Dover.

Lear having by some chance escaped from the guardians which the good earl of Kent had put over him to take care of him in his lunacy, was found by some of Cordelia's train, wandering about the fields near Dover, in a pitiable condition, stark mad and singing aloud to himself, with a crown upon his head which he had made of straw, and nettles, and other wild weeds that he had picked up in the corn-fields. By the advice of the physicians, Cordelia, though earnestly desirous of seeing her father, was prevailed upon to put off the meeting, till, by sleep and the operation of herbs which they gave him, he should be restored to greater composure. By the aid of these skilful physicians, to whom Cordelia promised all her gold and jewels for the recovery of the old king, Lear was soon in a condition to see his daughter.

A tender sight it was to see the meeting between this father and daughter: to see the struggles between the joy of this poor old king at beholding again his once darling child, and the shame at receiving such filial kindness from her whom he had cast off for so small a fault in his displeasure; both these passions struggling with the remains of his malady, which in his half-crazed brain sometimes made him that he scarce remembered where he was, or who it was that so kindly kissed him and spoke to him: and then he would beg the standers-by not to laugh at him, if he were mistaken in thinking this lady to be his daughter Cordelia! And then to see him fall on his knees to beg pardon of his child; and she, good lady, kneeling all the while to ask a blessing of him, and telling him that it did not become him to kneel, but it was her duty, for she was his child, his true and very child Cordelia! And she kissed him (as she said) to kiss away all her sisters' unkindness, and said that they might be ashamed of themselves, to turn their old kind father with his white beard out into the cold air, when her enemy's dog, though it had bit her (as she prettily expressed it), should have staid by her fire such a night as that, and warmed himself. And she told her father how she had come from France with purpose to bring him assistance; and he said, that she must forget and forgive, for he was old and foolish, and did not know what he did; but that to be sure she had great cause not to love him, but her sisters had none. And Cordelia said, that she had no cause, no more than they had.

So we will leave this old king in the protection of his dutiful and loving child, where, by the help of sleep and medicine, she and her physicians at length succeeded in winding up the untuned and jarring senses which the cruelty of his other daughters had so violently shaken. Let us return to say a word or two about those cruel daughters.

These monsters of ingratitude, who had been so false to their old father, could not be expected to prove more faithful to their own husbands. They soon grew tired of paying even the appearance of duty and affection, and in an open way shewed they had fixed their loves upon another. It happened that the object of their guilty loves was the same. It was Edmund, a natural son of the late earl of Gloucester, who by his treacheries had succeeded in disinheriting his brother Edgar the lawful heir from his earldom, and by his wicked practices was now earl himself: a wicked man, and a fit object for the love of such wicked creatures as Gonerill and Regan. It falling out about this time that the duke of Cornwall, Regan's husband, died, Regan immediately declared her intention of wedding this earl of Gloucester, which rousing the jealousy of her sister, to whom as well as to Regan this wicked earl had at sundry times professed love, Gonerill found means to make away with her sister by poison: but being detected in her practices, and imprisoned by her husband the duke of Albany, for this deed, and for her guilty passion for the earl which had come to his ears, she in a fit of disappointed love and rage shortly put an end to her own life. Thus the justice of Heaven at last overtook these wicked daughters.

While the eyes of all men were upon this event, admiring the justice displayed in their deserved deaths, the same eyes were suddenly taken off from this sight to admire at the mysterious ways of the same power in the melancholy fate of the young and virtuous daughter, the lady Cordelia, whose good deeds did seem to deserve a more fortunate conclusion: but it is an awful truth, that innocence and piety are not always successful in this world. The forces which Gonerill and Regan had sent out under the command of the bad earl of Gloucester were victorious, and Cordelia by the practices of this wicked earl, who did not like that any should stand between him and the throne, ended her life in prison. Thus, Heaven took this innocent lady to itself in her young years, after shewing her to the world an illustrious example of filial duty. Lear did not long survive this kind child.

Before he died, the good earl of Kent, who had still attended his old master's steps from the first of his daughters' ill usage to this sad period of his decay, tried to make him understand that it was he who had followed him under the name of Caius; but Lear's care-crazed brain at that time could not comprehend how that could be, or how Kent and Caius could be the same person: so Kent thought it needless to trouble him with explanations at such a time; and Lear soon after expiring, this faithful servant to the king, between age and grief for his old master's vexations, soon followed him to the grave.

How the judgment of Heaven overtook the bad earl of

Gloucester, whose treasons were discovered, and himself slain in single combat with his brother, the lawful earl; and how Gonerill's husband, the duke of Albany, who was innocent of the death of Cordelia, and had never encouraged his lady in her wicked proceedings against her father, ascended the throne of Britain after the death of Lear, is needless here to narrate; Lear and his Three Daughters being dead, whose adventures alone concern our story.

MACBETH

When Duncan the Meek reigned king of Scotland, there lived a great thane, or lord, called Macbeth. This Macbeth was a near kinsman to the king, and in great esteem at court for his valour and conduct in the wars; an example of which he had lately given, in defeating a rebel army assisted by the troops of Norway in terrible numbers.

The two Scottish generals, Macbeth and Banquo, returning victorious from this great battle, their way lay over a blasted heath, where they were stopped by the strange appearance of three figures, like women, except that they had beards, and their withered skins and wild attire made them look not like any earthly creatures. Macbeth first addressed them, when they, seemingly offended, laid each one her choppy finger upon her skinny lips, in token of silence: and the first of them saluted Macbeth with the title of thane of Glamis. The general was not a little startled to find himself known by such creatures; but how much more, when the second of them followed up that salute by giving him the title of thane of Cawdor, to which honour he had no pretensions! and again the third bid him 'All hail! king that shalt be hereafter.' Such a prophetic greeting might well amaze him, who knew that while the king's sons lived he could not hope to succeed to the throne. Then turning to Banquo, they pronounced him, in a sort of riddling terms, to be *lesser than Macbeth and greater! not so happy, but much happier!* and prophesied that though he should never reign, yet his sons after him should be kings in Scotland. They then turned into air, and vanished: by which the generals knew them to be the weird sisters, or witches.

While they stood pondering on the strangeness of this adventure,

The Witches Cauldron.

there arrived certain messengers from the king, who were empowered by him to confer upon Macbeth the dignity of thane of Cawdor. An event so miraculously corresponding with the prediction of the witches astonished Macbeth, and he stood wrapt in amazement, unable to make reply to the messengers: and in that point of time swelling hopes arose in his mind, that the prediction of the third witch might in like manner have its accomplishment, and that he should one day reign king in Scotland.

Turning to Banquo, he said, 'Do you not hope that your children shall be kings, when what the witches promised to me has so wonderfully come to pass?' 'That hope,' answered the general, 'might enkindle you to aim at the throne; but oftentimes these ministers of darkness tell us truths in little things, to betray us into deeds of greatest consequence.'

But the wicked suggestions of the witches had sunk too deep into the mind of Macbeth, to allow him to attend to the warnings of the good Banquo. From that time he bent all his thoughts how to compass the crown of Scotland.

Macbeth had a wife, to whom he communicated the strange prediction of the weird sisters, and its partial accomplishment. She was a bad ambitious woman, and so as her husband and herself could arrive at greatness, she cared not much by what means. She spurred on the reluctant purpose of Macbeth, who felt compunction at the thoughts of blood, and did not cease to represent the murder of the king as a step absolutely necessary to the fulfilment of the flattering prophecy.

It happened at this time that the king, who out of his royal condescension would oftentimes visit his principal nobility upon gracious terms, came to Macbeth's house, attended by his two sons, Malcolm and Donalbain, and a numerous train of thanes and attendants, the more to honour Macbeth for the triumphal success of his wars.

The castle of Macbeth was pleasantly situated, and the air about it was sweet and wholesome, which appeared by the nests which the martlet, or swallow, had built under all the jutting friezes and buttresses of the building, wherever it found a place of advantage: for where those birds most breed and haunt, the air is observed to be delicate. The king entered, well pleased with the place, and not less so with the attentions and respect of his honoured hostess, lady Macbeth, who had the art of covering treacherous purposes with

97

smiles; and could look like the innocent flower, while she was indeed the serpent under it.

The king, being tired with his journey, went early to bed, and in his state-room two grooms of his chamber (as was the custom) slept beside him. He had been unusually pleased with his reception, and had made presents, before he retired, to his principal officers; and among the rest, had sent a rich diamond to lady Macbeth, greeting her by the name of his most kind hostess.

Now was the middle of the night, when over half the world nature seems dead, and wicked dreams abuse men's minds asleep, and none but the wolf and the murderer is abroad. This was the time when lady Macbeth waked to plot the murder of the king. She would not have undertaken a deed so abhorrent to her sex, but that she feared her husband's nature, that it was too full of the milk of human kindness, to do a contrived murder. She knew him to be ambitious, but withal to be scrupulous, and not yet prepared for that height of crime which commonly in the end accompanies inordinate ambition. She had won him to consent to the murder, but she doubted his resolution: and she feared that the natural tenderness of his disposition (more humane than her own) would come between, and defeat the purpose. So with her own hands armed with a dagger, she approached the king's bed; having taken care to ply the grooms of his chamber so with wine, that they slept intoxicated, and careless of their charge. There lay Duncan, in a sound sleep after the fatigues of his journey, and as she viewed him earnestly, there was something in his face, as he slept, which resembled her own father; and she had not the courage to proceed.

She returned to confer with her husband. His resolution had begun to stagger. He considered that there were strong reasons against the deed. In the first place, he was not only a subject, but a near kinsman to the king; and he had been his host and entertainer that day, whose duty by the laws of hospitality it was to shut the door against his murderers, not bear the knife himself. Then he considered how just and merciful a king this Duncan had been, how clear of offence to his subjects, how loving to his nobility, and in particular to him; that such kings are the peculiar care of Heaven, and their subjects doubly bound to revenge their deaths. Besides, by the favours of the king, Macbeth stood high in the opinion of all sorts of men, and how would those honours be stained by the reputation of so foul a murder!

In these conflicts of the mind lady Macbeth found her husband, inclining to the better part, and resolving to proceed no further. But she being a woman not easily shaken from her evil purpose, began to pour in at his ears words which infused a portion of her own spirit into his mind, assigning reason upon reason why he should not shrink from what he had undertaken; how easy the deed was; how soon it would be over; and how the action of one short night would give to all their nights and days to come sovereign sway and royalty! Then she threw contempt on his change of purpose, and accused him of fickleness and cowardice; and declared that she had given suck, and knew how tender it was to love the babe that milked her, but she would, while it was smiling in her face, have plucked it from her breast, and dashed its brains out, if she had so sworn to do it, as he had sworn to perform that murder. Then she added, how practicable it was to lay the guilt of the deed upon the drunken sleepy grooms. And with the valour of her tongue she so chastised his sluggish resolutions, that he once more summoned up courage to the bloody business.

So, taking the dagger in his hand, he softly stole in the dark to the room where Duncan lay; and as he went, he thought he saw another dagger in the air, with the handle towards him, and on the blade and at the point of it drops of blood: but when he tried to grasp at it, it was nothing but air, a mere phantasm proceeding from his own hot and oppressed brain and the business he had in hand.

Getting rid of this fear, he entered the king's room, whom he dispatched with one stroke of his dagger. Just as he had done the murder, one of the grooms, who slept in the chamber, laughed in his sleep, and the other cried 'Murder,' which woke them both: but they said a short prayer; one of them said, 'God bless us! ' and the other answered 'Amen;' and addressed themselves to sleep again. Macbeth, who stood listening to them, tried to say, 'Amen,' when the fellow said, 'God bless us! ' but, though he had most need of a blessing, the word stuck in his throat, and he could not pronounce it.

Again he thought he heard a voice which cried, 'Sleep no more: Macbeth doth murder sleep, the innocent sleep, that nourishes life.' Still it cried, 'Sleep no more,' to all the house. 'Glamis hath murdered sleep, and therefore Cawdor shall sleep no more, Macbeth shall sleep no more.'

With such horrible imaginations, Macbeth returned to his listening wife, who began to think he had failed of his purpose, and that the deed was somehow frustrated. He came in so distracted a state, that she reproached him with his want of firmness, and sent him to wash his hands of the blood which stained them, while she took his dagger, with purpose to stain the cheeks of the grooms with blood, to make it seem their guilt.

Morning came, and with it the discovery of the murder, which could not be concealed; and though Macbeth and his lady made great show of grief, and the proofs against the grooms (the dagger being produced against them and their faces smeared with blood) were sufficiently strong, yet the entire suspicion fell upon Macbeth, whose inducements to such a deed were so much more forcible than such poor silly grooms could be supposed to have; and Duncan's two sons fled. Malcolm, the eldest, sought for refuge in the English court; and the youngest, Donalbain, made his escape to Ireland.

The king's sons, who should have succeeded him, having thus vacated the throne, Macbeth as next heir was crowned king, and thus the prediction of the weird sisters was literally accomplished.

Though placed so high, Macbeth and his queen could not forget the prophecy of the weird sisters, that, though Macbeth should be king, yet not his children, but the children of Banquo, should be kings after him. The thought of this, and that they had defiled their hands with blood, and done so great crimes, only to place the posterity of Banquo upon the throne, so rankled within them, that they determined to put to death both Banquo and his son, to make void the predictions of the weird sisters, which in their own case had been so remarkably brought to pass.

For this purpose they made a great supper, to which they invited all the chief thanes; and, among the rest, with marks of particular respect, Banquo and his son Fleance were invited. The way by which Banquo was to pass to the palace at night, was beset by murderers appointed by Macbeth, who stabbed Banquo; but in the scuffle Fleance escaped. From that Fleance descended a race of monarchs who afterwards filled the Scottish throne, ending with James the sixth of Scotland and the first of England, under whom the two crowns of England and Scotland were united.

At supper the queen, whose manners were in the highest degree affable and royal, played the hostess with a gracefulness and attention which conciliated every one present, and Macbeth discoursed freely with his thanes and nobles, saying, that all that was honourable in the country was under his roof, if he had but his good friend Banquo present, whom yet he hoped he should rather have to chide for neglect, than to lament for any mischance. Just at these words the ghost of Banquo, whom he had caused to be murdered, entered the room, and placed himself on the chair which Macbeth was about to occupy. Though Macbeth was a bold man, and one that could have faced the devil without trembling, at this horrible sight his cheeks turned white with fear, and he stood quite unmanned with his eyes fixed upon the ghost. His queen and all the nobles, who saw nothing, but perceived him gazing (as they thought) upon an empty chair, took it for a fit of distraction; and she reproached him, whispering that it was but the same fancy which had made him see the dagger in the air, when he was about to kill Duncan. But Macbeth continued to see the ghost, and gave no heed to all they could say, while he addressed it with distracted words, yet so significant, that his queen, fearing the dreadful secret would be disclosed, in great haste dismissed the guests, excusing the infirmity of Macbeth as a disorder he was often troubled with.

To such dreadful fancies Macbeth was subject. His queen and he had their sleeps afflicted with terrible dreams, and the blood of Banquo troubled them not more than the escape of Fleance, whom now they looked upon as father to a line of kings, who should keep their posterity out of the throne. With these miserable thoughts they found no peace, and Macbeth determined once more to seek out the weird sisters, and know from them the worst.

He sought them in a cave upon the heath, where they, who knew by foresight of his coming, were engaged in preparing their dreadful charms, by which they conjured up infernal spirits to reveal to them futurity. Their horrid ingredients were toads, bats, and serpents, the eye of a newt, and the tongue of a dog, the leg of a lizard, and the wing of the night-owl, the scale of a dragon, the tooth of a wolf, the maw of the ravenous salt-sea shark, the mummy of a witch, the root of the poisonous hemlock (this to have effect must be digged in the dark), the gall of a goat, and the liver of a Jew, with slips of the yew tree that roots itself in graves, and the finger of a dead child: all these were set on to boil in a great kettle, or cauldon, which, as fast as it grew too hot, was cooled with a baboon's blood: to these they poured in the blood of a sow that had eaten her young, and they threw into the flame the grease that had sweaten from a murderer's gibbet. By these charms they bound the infernal spirits to answer their questions.

It was demanded of Macbeth, whether he would have his doubts resolved by them, or by their masters, the spirits. He, nothing daunted by the dreadful ceremonies which he saw, boldly answered, 'Where are they? let me see them.' And they called the spirits, which were three. And the first arose in the likeness of an armed head, and he called Macbeth by name, and bid him beware of the thane of Fife; for which caution Macbeth thanked him: for Macbeth had entertained a jealousy of Macduff, the thane of Fife.

And the second spirit arose in the likeness of a bloody child, and he called Macbeth by name, and bid him have no fear, but laugh to scorn the power of man, for none of woman born should have power to hurt him: and he advised him to be bloody, bold, and resolute. 'Then live, Macduff! ' cried the king; 'what need I fear of thee? but yet I will make assurance doubly sure. Thou shalt not live; that I may tell pale-hearted fear it lies, and sleep in spite of thunder.'

That spirit being dismissed, a third arose in the form of a child crowned, with a tree in his hand. He called Macbeth by name, and comforted him against conspiracies, saying, that he should never be vanquished, until the wood of Birnam to Dunsinane-Hill should come against him. 'Sweet bodements! good! ' cried Macbeth; 'who can unfix the forest, and move it from its earthbound roots? I see I shall live the usual period of man's life, and not be cut off by a violent death. But my heart throbs to know one thing. Tell me, if your art can tell so much, if Banquo's issue shall ever reign in this kingdom?' Here the cauldron sank into the ground, and a noise of music was heard, and eight shadows, like kings, passed by Macbeth, and Banquo last, who bore a glass which shewed the figures of many more, and Banquo all bloody smiled upon Macbeth, and pointed to them; by which Macbeth knew, that these were the posterity of Banquo, who should reign after him in Scotland; and the witches, with a sound of soft music, and with dancing, making a shew of duty and welcome to Macbeth, vanished. And from this time the thoughts of Macbeth were all bloody and dreadful.

The first thing he heard when he got out of the witches' cave, was, that Macduff, thane of Fife, had fled to England, to join the army which was forming against him under Malcolm, the eldest son of the late king, with intent to displace Macbeth, and set Malcolm, the right heir, upon the throne. Macbeth, stung with rage, set upon the castle of Macduff, and put his wife and children, whom the thane had left behind, to the sword, and extended the slaughter to all who claimed the least relationship to Macduff.

These and such-like deeds alienated the minds of all his chief nobility from him. Such as could, fled to join with Malcolm and Macduff, who were now approaching with a powerful army which they had raised in England; and the rest secretly wished success to their arms, though for fear of Macbeth they could take no active part. His recruits went on slowly. Every body hated the tyrant, nobody loved or honoured him, but all suspected him, and he began to envy the condition of Duncan whom he had murdered, who slept soundly in his grave, against whom treason had done its worst: steel nor poison, domestic malice nor foreign levies, could hurt him any longer.

While these things were acting, the queen, who had been the sole partner in his wickedness, in whose bosom he could sometimes seek a momentary repose from those terrible dreams which afflicted them both nightly, died, it is supposed by her own hands, unable to bear the remorse of guilt, and public hate; by which event he was left alone, without a soul to love or care for him, or a friend to whom he could confide his wicked purposes.

He grew careless of life, and wished for death; but the near approach of Malcolm's army roused in him what remained of his ancient courage, and he determined to die (as he expressed it) 'with armour on his back.' Besides this, the hollow promises of the witches had filled him with false confidence, and he remembered the sayings of the spirits, that none of woman born was to hurt him, and that he was never to be vanquished till Birnam wood should come to Dunsinane, which he thought could never be. So he shut himself up in his castle, whose impregnable strength was such as defied a siege: here he sullenly waited the approach of Malcolm. When, upon a day, there came a messenger to him, pale and shaking with fear, almost unable to report that which he had seen: for he averred, that as he stood upon his watch on the hill, he looked towards Birnam, and to his thinking the wood began to move! 'Liar and slave' cried Macbeth; 'if thou speakest false, thou shalt hang alive upon the next tree, till famine end thee. If thy tale be true, I care not if thou dost as much by me:' for Macbeth now began to faint in resolution, and to doubt the

103

equivocal speeches of the spirits. He was not to fear till Birnam wood should come to Dunsinane: and now a wood did move! 'However,' said he, 'if this which he avouches be true, let us arm and out. There is no flying hence, nor staying here. I begin to be weary of the sun, and wish my life at an end.' With these desperate speeches he sallied forth upon the besiegers, who had now come up to the castle.

The strange appearance, which had given the messenger an idea of a wood moving, is easily solved. When the besieging army marched through the wood of Birnam, Malcolm, like a skilful general, instructed his soldiers to hew down every one a bough and bear it before him, by way of concealing the true numbers of his host. This marching of the soldiers with boughs had at a distance the appearance which had frightened the messenger. Thus were the words of the spirit brought to pass, in a sense different from that in which Macbeth had understood them, and one great hold of his confidence was gone.

And now a severe skirmishing took place, in which Macbeth, though feebly supported by those who called themselves his friends, but in reality hated the tyrant and inclined to the party of Malcolm and Macduff, yet fought with the extreme of rage and valour, cutting to pieces all who were opposed to him, till he came to where Macduff was fighting. Seeing Macduff, and remembering the caution of the spirit who had counselled him to avoid Macduff above all men, he would have turned, but Macduff, who had been seeking him through the whole fight, opposed his turning, and a fierce contest ensued; Macduff giving him many foul reproaches for the murder of his wife and children. Macbeth, whose soul was charged enough with blood of that family already, would still have declined the combat; but Macduff still urged him to it, calling him tyrant, murderer, hell-hound, and villain.

Then Macbeth remembered the words of the spirit, how none of woman born should hurt him; and smiling confidently he said to Macduff, 'Thou losest thy labour, Macduff. As easily thou mayest impress the air with thy sword, as make me vulnerable. I bear a charmed life, which must not yield to one of woman born.'

'Despair thy charm,' said Macduff, 'and let that lying spirit whom thou hast served, tell thee, that Macduff was never born of woman, never as the ordinary manner of men is to be born, but was untimely taken from his mother.'

'Accursed be the tongue which tells me so,' said the trembling Macbeth, who felt his last hold of confidence give way; 'and let never man in future believe the lying equivocations of witches and juggling spirits, who deceive us in words which have double senses, and while they keep their promise literally, disappoint our hopes with a different meaning. I will not fight with thee.'

'Then, live!' said the scornful Macduff; 'we will have a show of thee, as men shew monsters, and a painted board, on which shall be written, Here men may see the tyrant!'

'Never,' said Macbeth, whose courage returned with despair; 'I will not live to kiss the ground before young Malcolm's feet, and to be baited with the curses of the rabble. Though Birnam wood be come to Dunsinane, and thou opposed to me who wast never born of woman, yet will I try the last.' With these frantic words he threw himself upon Macduff, who, after a severe struggle in the end overcame him, and cutting off his head, made a present of it to the young and lawful king, Malcolm; who took upon him the government which by the machinations of the usurper he had so long been deprived of, and ascended the throne of Duncan the Meek amid the acclamations of the nobles and the people.

TIMON OF ATHENS

Timon, a lord of Athens, in the enjoyment of a princely fortune, affected a humour of liberality which knew no limits. His almost infinite wealth could not flow in so fast, but he poured it out faster upon all sorts and degrees of people. Not the poor only tasted of his bounty, but great lords did not disdain to rank themselves among his dependants and followers. His table was resorted to by all the luxurious feasters, and his house was open to all comers and goers at Athens. His large wealth combined with his free and prodigal nature to subdue all hearts to his love; men of all minds and dispositions tendered their services to lord Timon, from the glass-faced flatterer, whose face reflects as in a mirror the present humour of his patron, to the rough and unbending cynic, who affecting a contempt of men's persons, and an indifference to worldly things, yet could not stand out against the gracious manners and munificent soul of lord Timon, but would come (against his

The Last Entertainment of Timon.

nature) to partake of his royal entertainments, and return most rich in his own estimation if he had received a nod or a salutation from Timon.

If a poet had composed a work which wanted a recommendatory introduction to the world, he had no more to do but to dedicate it to lord Timon, and the poem was sure of sale, besides a present purse from the patron, and daily access to his house and table. If a painter had a picture to dispose of, he had only to take it to lord Timon, and pretend to consult his taste as to the merits of it; nothing more was wanting to persuade the liberal-hearted lord to buy it. If a jeweller had a stone of price, or a mercer rich costly stuffs, which for their costliness lay upon his hands, lord Timon's house was a ready mart always open, where they might get off their wares or their jewellery at any price, and the good natured lord would thank them into the bargain, as if they had done him a piece of courtesy in letting him have the refusal of such precious commodities. So that by this means his house was thronged with superfluous purchases, of no use but to swell uneasy and ostentatious pomp; and his person was still more inconveniently beset with a crowd of these idle visitors, lying poets, painters, sharking tradesmen, lords, ladies, needy courtiers, and expectants, who continually filled his lobbies, raining their fulsome flatteries in whispers in his ears, sacrificing to him with adulation as to a God, making sacred the very stirrup by which he mounted his horse, and seeming as though they drank the free air but through his permission and bounty.

Some of these daily dependents were young men of birth, who (their means not answering to their extravagance) had been put in prison by creditors, and redeemed thence by lord Timon; these young prodigals thenceforward fastened upon his lordship, as if by common sympathy he were necessarily endeared to all such spendthrifts and loose livers, who not being able to follow him in his wealth, found it easier to copy him in prodigality and copious spending of what was not their own. One of these flesh-flies was Ventidius, for whose debts unjustly contracted Timon but lately had paid down the sum of five talents.

But among this confluence, this great flood of visitors, none were more conspicuous than the makers of presents and givers of gifts. It was fortunate for these men, if Timon took a fancy to a dog, or a horse, or any piece of cheap furniture which was theirs. The thing so praised, whatever it was, was sure to be sent the next morning with the compliments of the giver for lord Timon's acceptance, and apologies for the unworthiness of the gift; and this dog or horse, or whatever it might be, did not fail to produce, from Timon's bounty, who would not be outdone in gifts, perhaps twenty dogs or horses, certainly presents of far richer worth, as these pretended donors knew well enough, and that their false presents were but the putting out of so much money at large and speedy interest. In this way lord Lucius had lately sent to Timon a present of four milk-white horses trapped in silver, which this cunning lord had observed Timon upon some occasion to commend; and another lord, Lucullus, had bestowed upon him in the same pretended way of free gift a brace of greyhounds, whose make and fleetness Timon had been heard to admire; these presents the easy-hearted lord accepted without suspicion of the dishonest views of the presenters: and the givers of course were rewarded with some rich return, a diamond or some jewel of twenty times the value of their false and mercenary donation.

Sometimes these creatures would go to work in a more direct way, and with gross and palpable artifice, which yet the credulous Timon was too blind to see, would affect to admire and praise something that Timon possessed, a bargain that he had bought, or some late purchase, which was sure to draw from this yielding and soft-hearted lord a gift of the thing commended, for no service in the world done for it but the easy expence of a little cheap and obvious flattery. In this way Timon but the other day had given to one of these mean lords the bay courser which he himself rode upon, because his lordship had been pleased to say that it was a handsome beast and went well; and Timon knew that no man ever justly praised what he did not wish to possess. For lord Timon weighed his friends' affection with his own, and so fond was he of bestowing, that he could have dealt kingdoms to these supposed friends, and never have been weary.

Not that Timon's wealth all went to enrich these wicked flatterers: he could do noble and praise-worthy actions; and when a servant of his once loved the daughter of a rich Athenian, but could not hope to obtain her by reason that in wealth and rank the maid was so far above him, lord Timon freely bestowed upon his servant three Athenian talents, to make his fortune equal with the dowry which the father of the young maid demanded of him who should be her husband. But for the most part, knaves and parasites had the command of his fortune, false friends whom he did not know to be such, but, because they flocked around his person, he thought they must needs love him; and because they smiled, and flattered him, he thought surely that his conduct was approved by all the wise and good. And when he was feasting in the midst of all these flatterers and mock friends, when they were eating him up, and draining his fortunes dry with large draughts of richest wines drunk to his health and prosperity, he could not perceive the difference of a friend from a flatterer, but to his deluded eyes (made proud with the sight) it seemed a precious comfort to have so many, like brothers commanding one another's fortunes (though it was his own fortune which paid all the cost), and with joy they would run over at the spectacle of such, as it appeared to him, truly festive and fraternal meeting.

But while he thus outwent the very heart of kindness, and poured out his bounty, as if Plutus, the god of gold, had been but his steward; while thus he proceeded without care or stop, so senseless of expence that he would neither enquire how he could maintain it, nor cease his wild flow or riot; his riches, which were not infinite, must needs melt away before a prodigality which knew no limits. But who should tell him so? his flatterers? they had an interest in shutting his eyes. In vain did his honest steward Flavius try to represent to him his condition, laying his accounts before him, begging of him, praying of him, with an importunity that on any other occasion would have been unmannerly in a servant, beseeching him with tears, to look into the state of his affairs. Timon would still put him off, and turn the discourse to something else; for nothing is so deaf to remonstrance as riches turned to poverty, nothing is so unwilling to believe its situation, nothing so incredulous to its own true state, and hard to give credit to a reverse. Often had this good steward, this honest creature, when all the rooms of Timon's great house have been choked up with riotous feeders at his master's cost, when the floors have wept with drunken spilling of wine, and every apartment has blazed with lights and resounded with music and feasting, often had he retired by himself to some solitary spot, and wept faster than the wine ran from the wasteful casks within, to see the mad bounty of his lord, and to think, when the means were gone which bought him praises from all sorts of people, how quickly the breath would be gone of which the praise was made; praises won in feasting would be lost in fasting, and at one cloud of winter-showers these flies would disappear.

But now the time was come that Timon could shut his ears no longer to the representations of this faithful steward. Money must be had; and when he ordered Flavius to sell some of his land for that purpose, Flavius informed him, what he had in vain endeavoured at several times before to make him listen to, that most of his land was already sold or forfeited, and that all he possessed at present was not enough to pay the one half of what he owed. Struck with wonder at this presentation, Timon hastily replied, 'My lands extended from Athens to Lacedemon.' 'O my good lord,' said Flavius, 'the world is but a world, and has bounds; were it all yours to give in a breath, how quickly were it gone.'

Timon consoled himself that no villainous bounty had yet come from him, that if he had given his wealth away unwisely, it had not been bestowed to feed his vices, but to cherish his friends; and he bade the kind-hearted steward (who was weeping) to take comfort in the assurance that his master could never lack means, while he had so many noble friends; and this infatuated lord persuaded himself that he had nothing to do but to send and borrow, to use every man's fortune (that had ever tasted his bounty) in this extremity, as freely as his own. Then with a cheerful look, as if confident of the trial, he severally dispatched messengers to lord Lucius, to lords Lucullus and Sempronius, men upon whom he had lavished his gifts in past times without measure or moderation; and to Ventidius, whom he had lately released out of prison by paying his debts, and who by the death of his father was now come into the possession of an ample fortune, and well enabled to requite Timon's courtesy; to request of Ventidius the return of those five talents which he had paid for him, and of each of those noble lords the loan of fifty talents: nothing doubting that their gratitude would supply his wants (if he needed it) to the amount of five hundred times fifty talents.

Lucullus was the first applied to. This mean lord had been dreaming over-night of a silver bason and cup, and when Timon's servant was announced, his sordid mind suggested to him that this was surely a making out of his dream, and that Timon had sent him such a present: but when he understood the truth of the matter, and that Timon wanted money, the quality of his faint and watery friendship shewed itself, for with many protestations he vowed to the servant that he had long foreseen the ruin of his master's affairs, and many a time had he come to dinner, to tell him of it, and had come again to supper, to try to persuade him to spend less, but he would take no counsel nor warning by his coming: and true it was that he had been a constant attender (as he said) at Timon's feasts, as he had in greater things tasted his bounty, but that he ever came with that intent, or gave good counsel or reproof to Timon, was a base unworthy lie, which he suitably followed up with meanly offering the servant a bribe, to go home to his master and tell him that he had not found Lucullus at home.

As little success had the messenger who was sent to lord Lucius. This lying lord, who was full of Timon's meat, and enriched almost to bursting with Timon's costly presents, when he found the wind changed, and the fountain of so much bounty suddenly stopt, at first could hardly believe it; but on its being confirmed, he affected great regret that he should not have it in his power to serve lord Timon, for unfortunately (which was a base falsehood) he had made a great purchase the day before, which had quite disfurnished him of the means at present; the more beast he, he called himself, to put it out of his power to serve so good a friend; and he counted it one of his greatest afflictions that his ability should fail him to pleasure such an honourable gentleman.

Who can call any man friend that dips in the same dish with him? just of this metal is every flatterer. In the recollection of every body Timon had been a father to this Lucius, had kept up his credit with his purse; Timon's money had gone to pay the wages of his servants, to pay the hire of the labourers who had sweat to build the fine houses which Lucius's pride had made necessary to him: yet, oh! the monster which man makes himself when he proves ungrateful! this Lucius now denied to Timon a sum, which, in respect of what Timon had bestowed on him, was less than charitable men afford to beggars.

Sempronius and every one of these mercenary lords to whom Timon applied in their turn, returned the same evasive answer or direct denial; even Ventidius, the redeemed and now rich Ventidius, refused to assist him with those five talents which Timon had not lent but generously given him in his distress.

Now was Timon as much avoided in his poverty, as he had been courted and resorted to in his riches. Now the same tongues which had been loudest in his praises, extolling him as bountiful, liberal, and open-handed, were not ashamed to censure that very bounty as folly, that liberality as profuseness, though it had shewn itself folly in nothing so truly as in the selection of such unworthy creatures as themselves for its objects. Now was Timon's princely mansion forsaken, and become a shunned and hated place, a place for men to pass by, not a place as formerly where every passenger must stop and taste of his wine and good cheer; now instead of being thronged with feasting and tumultuous guests, it was beset with impatient and clamorous creditors, usurers, extortioners, fierce and intolerable in their demands, pleading bonds, interest, mortgages, iron-hearted men that would take no denial nor putting off, that Timon's house was now his jail, where he could not pass, nor go in nor out for them; one demanding his due of fifty talents, another bringing in a bill of five thousand crowns, which if he would tell out his blood by drops, and pay them so, he had not enough in his body to discharge, drop by drop.

In this desperate and irremediable state (as it seemed) of his affairs, the eyes of all men were suddenly surprised at a new and incredible lustre which this setting sun put forth. Once more lord Timon proclaimed a feast, to which he invited his accustomed guests, lords, ladies, all that was great or fashionable in Athens. Lords Lucius and Lucullus came, Ventidius, Sempronius, and the rest. Who more sorry now than these fawning wretches, when they found (as they thought) that lord Timon's poverty was all pretence, and had been only put on to make trial of their loves, to think that they should not have seen through the artifice at the time, and have had the cheap credit of obliging his lordship? yet who more glad to find the fountain of that noble bounty, which they had thought dried up, still fresh and running? They came dissembling, protesting, expressing deepest sorrow and shame, that when his lordship sent to them, they should have been so unfortunate as to want the present means to oblige so honourable a friend. But Timon begged them not to give such trifles a thought, for he had altogether forgotten it. And these base fawning lords, though they had denied him money in his adversity, yet could not refuse their presence at this new blaze of his returning prosperity. For the swallow follows not summer more willingly than men of these dispositions follow the good fortunes of the great, nor more willingly leaves winter than these shrink from the first appearance of a reverse; such summer-birds are men. But now with music and state the banquet of smoking dishes was served up; and when the guests had a little done admiring whence the bankrupt Timon could find means to furnish so costly a feast, some doubting whether the scene which they saw was real, as scarce trusting their own eyes; at a signal given, the dishes were uncovered, and Timon's drift appeared: instead of those varieties and far-fetched dainties which they expected, that Timon's epicurean table in past times had so liberally presented, now appeared under the covers of these dishes a preparation more suitable to Timon's poverty, nothing but a little smoke and luke-warm water, fit feast for this knot of mouth-friends, whose professions were indeed smoke, and their hearts luke-warm and slippery as the water, with which Timon welcomed his astonished guests, bidding them, 'Uncover, dogs, and lap;' and before they could recover their surprise, sprinkling it in their faces, that they might have enough, and throwing dishes and all after them, who now ran huddling out, lords, ladies, with their caps snatched up in haste, a splendid confusion, Timon pursuing them, still calling them what they were, 'Smooth, smiling parasites, destroyers under the mask of courtesy, affable wolves, meek bears, fools of fortune, feast-friends, time-flies.' They, crowding out to avoid him, left the house more willingly than they had entered it; some losing their gowns and caps, and some their jewels in the hurry, all glad to escape out of the presence of such a mad lord, and the ridicule of his mock banquet.

This was the last feast which ever Timon made, and in it he took farewell of Athens and the society of men; for, after that, he betook himself to the woods, turning his back upon the hated city and upon all mankind, wishing the walls of that detestable city might sink, and the houses fall upon their owners, wishing all plagues which infest humanity, war, outrage, poverty, diseases, might fasten upon its inhabitants, praying the just gods to confound all Athenians, both young and old, high and low; so wishing, he went to the woods, where he said he should find the unkindest beast much kinder than those of his own species. He stripped himself naked, that he might retain no fashion of a man, and dug a cave to live in, and lived solitary in the manner of a beast, eating the wild roots, and drinking water, flying from the face of his kind, and choosing rather to herd with wild beasts, as more harmless and friendly than man.

What a change from lord Timon the rich, lord Timon the delight of mankind, to Timon the naked, Timon the man-hater! Where were his flatterers now? Where were his attendants and retinue? Would the bleak air, that boisterous servitor, be his chamberlain, to put his shirt on warm? Would those stiff trees, that had outlived the eagle, turn young and airy pages to him, to skip on his errands when he bade them? Would the cool brook, when it was iced with winter, administer to him his warm broths and caudles when sick of an over-night's surfeit? Or would the creatures that lived in those wild woods, come and lick his hand, and flatter him?

Here on a day, when he was digging for roots, his poor sustenance, his spade struck against something heavy, which proved to be gold, a great heap which some miser had probably buried in a time of alarm, thinking to have come again and taken it from its prison, but died before the opportunity had arrived, without making any man privy to the concealment; so it lay, doing neither good nor harm, in the bowels of the earth, its mother, as if it had never come from thence, till the accidental striking of Timon's spade against it once more brought it to light.

Here was a mass of treasure which if Timon had retained his old mind, was enough to have purchased him friends and flatterers again; but Timon was sick of the false world, and the sight of gold was poisonous to his eyes; and he would have restored it to the earth, but that, thinking of the infinite calamities which by means of gold happen to mankind, how the lucre of it causes robberies, oppression, injustice, briberies, violence and murder, among men, he had a pleasure in imagining (such a rooted hatred did he bear to his species) that out of this heap which in digging he had discovered, might arise some mischief to plague mankind. And some soldiers passing through the woods near to his cave at that instant, which proved to be a part of the troops of the Athenian captain Alcibiades, who upon some disgust taken against the senators of Athens (the Athenians were ever noted to be a thankless and ungrateful people, giving disgust to their generals and best friends), was marching at the head of the same triumphant army which he had formerly headed in their defence, to war against them; Timon, who liked their business well, bestowed upon their captain the gold to pay his soldiers, requiring no other service from him, than that he should with his conquering army lay Athens level with the ground, and burn, slay, kill all her inhabitants; not sparing the old men for their white beards, for (he said) they were usurers, nor the young children for their seeming innocent smiles, for those (he said) would live, if they grew up, to be traitors; but to steel his eyes and ears against any sights or sounds that might awaken compassion; and not to let the cries of virgins, babes, or mothers, hinder him from making one universal massacre of the city, but to confound them all in his conquest; and when he had conquered, he prayed that the gods would confound him also, the conqueror: so thoroughly did Timon hate Athens, Athenians, and all mankind.

While he lived in this forlorn state, leading a life more brutal than human, he was suddenly surprised one day with the appearance of a man standing in an admiring posture at the door of his cave. It was Flavius, the honest steward, whom love and zealous affection to his master had led to seek him out at his wretched dwelling, and to offer his services! and the first sight of his master, the once noble Timon, in that abject condition, naked as he was born, living in the manner of a beast among beasts, looking like his own sad ruins and a monument of decay, so affected this good servant, that he stood speechless, wrapt up in horror, and confounded. And when he found utterance at last to his words, they were so choaked with tears, that Timon had much ado to know him again, or to make out who it was that had come (so contrary to the experience he had had of mankind) to offer him service in extremity. And being in the form and shape of a man, he suspected him for a traitor, and his tears for false; but the good servant by so many tokens confirmed the truth of his fidelity, and made it clear that nothing but love and zealous duty to his once dear master had brought him there, that Timon was forced to confess that the world contained one honest man; yet, being in the shape and form of a man, he could not look upon his man's face without abhorrence, or hear words uttered from his man's lips without loathing; and this singly honest man was forced to depart, because he was a man, and because, with a heart more gentle and compassionate than is usual to man, he bore man's detested form and outward feature.

But greater visitants than a poor steward were about to interrupt the savage quiet of Timon's solitude. For now the day was come when the ungrateful lords of Athens sorely repented the injustice which they had done to the noble Timon. For Alcibiades, like an incensed wild boar, was raging at the walls of their city, and with his hot siege threatened to lay fair Athens in the dust. And now the memory of lord Timon's former prowess and military conduct came fresh into their forgetful minds, for Timon had been their general in past times, and was a valiant and expert soldier, who alone of all the Athenians was deemed able to cope with a besieging army, such as then threatened them, or to drive back the furious approaches of Alcibiades.

A deputation of the senators was chosen in this emergency to wait upon Timon. To him they come in their extremity, to whom, when he was in extremity, they had shewn but small regard; as if they presumed upon his gratitude whom they had disobliged, and had derived a claim to his courtesy from their own most discourteous and unpiteous treatment.

Now they earnestly beseech him, implore him with tears, to return and save that city, from which their ingratitude had so lately driven him; now they offer him riches, power, dignities, satisfaction for past injuries, and public honours and the public love; their persons, lives and fortunes, to be at his disposal, if he will but come back and save them. But Timon the naked, Timon the man-hater, was no longer lord Timon, the lord of bounty, the flower of valour, their defence in war, their ornament in peace. If Alcibiades killed his countrymen, Timon cared not. If he sacked fair Athens, and slew her old men and her infants, Timon would rejoice. So he told them; and that there was not a knife in the unruly camp which he did not prize above the reverendest throat in Athens.

This was all the answer he vouchsafed to the weeping disappointed senators; only at parting, he bade them commend him to his countrymen, and tell them, that to ease them of their griefs and anxieties, and to prevent the consequences of fierce Alcibiades' wrath, there was yet a way left, which he would teach them, for he had yet so much affection left for his dear countrymen as to be willing to do them a kindness before his death. These words a little revived the senators, who hoped that his kindness for their city was returning. Then Timon told them that he had a tree, which grew near his cave, which he should shortly have occasion to cut down, and he invited all his friends in Athens, high or low, of what degree soever, who wished to shun affliction, to come and take a taste of his tree before he cut it down; meaning, that they might come and hang themselves on it, and escape affliction that way.

And this was the last courtesy, of all his noble bounties, which Timon shewed to mankind, and this the last sight of him which his countrymen had: for not many days after, a poor soldier, passing by the sea-beach, which was at a little distance from the woods which Timon frequented, found a tomb on the verge of the sea, with an inscription upon it, purporting that it was the grave of Timon the man-hater, who 'While he lived, did hate all living men, and dying, wished a plague might consume all caitiffs left! '

Whether he finished his life by violence, or whether mere distaste of life and the loathing he had for mankind brought Timon to his conclusion, was not clear, yet all men admired the fitness of his epitaph, and the consistency of his end; dying, as he had lived, a hater of mankind: and some there were who fancied a conceit in the very choice which he had made of the sea-beach for his place of burial, where the vast sea might weep for ever upon his grave, as in contempt of the transient and shallow tears of hypocritical and deceitful mankind.

ROMEO AND JULIET

The two chief families in Verona were the rich Capulets and the Mountagues. There had been an old quarrel between these families, which was grown to such a height, and so deadly was the enmity between them, that it extended to the remotest kindred, to the followers and retainers of both sides, insomuch that a servant of the house of Mountague could not meet a servant of the house of Capulet, nor a Capulet encounter with a Mountague by chance, but fierce words and sometimes bloodshed ensued; and frequent were the brawls from such accidental meetings, which disturbed the happy quiet of Verona's streets.

Old lord Capulet made a great supper, to which many fair ladies and many noble guests were invited. All the admired beauties of Verona were present, and all comers were made welcome if they were not of the house of Mountague. At this feast of Capulets, Rosaline, beloved of Romeo, son to the old lord Mountague, was present; and though it was dangerous for a Mountague to be seen in this assembly, yet Benvolio, a friend of Romeo, persuaded the young lord to go to this assembly in the disguise of a mask, that he might see his Rosaline, and seeing her compare her with some choice beauties of Verona, who (he said) would make him think

117

his swan a crow. Romeo had small faith in Benvolio's words; nevertheless, for the love of Rosaline, he was persuaded to go. For Romeo was a sincere and passionate lover, and one that lost his sleep for love, and fled society to be alone, thinking on Rosaline, who disdained him, and never requited his love with the least show of courtesy or affection; and Benvolio wished to cure his friend of this love by shewing him diversity of ladies and company. To this feast of Capulets then young Romeo with Benvolio and their friend Mercutio went masked. Old Capulet bid them welcome, and told them that ladies who had their toes unplagued with corns would dance with them. And the old man was light-hearted and merry, and said that he had worn a mask when he was young, and could have told a whispering tale in a fair lady's ear. And they fell to dancing, and Romeo was suddenly struck with the exceeding beauty of a lady who danced there, who seemed to him to teach the torches to burn bright, and her beauty to shew by night like a rich jewel worn by a blackamoor: beauty too rich for use, too dear for earth! like a snowy dove trooping with crows (he said), so richly did her beauty and perfections shine above the ladies her companions. While he uttered these praises, he was overheard by Tybalt, a nephew of lord Capulet, who knew him by his voice to be Romeo. And this Tybalt, being of a fiery and passionate temper, could not endure that a Mountague should come under cover of a mask, to fleer and scorn (as he said) at their solemnities. And he stormed and raged exceedingly, and would have struck young Romeo dead. But his uncle, the old lord Capulet, would not suffer him to do any injury at that time, both out of respect to his guests, and because Romeo had borne himself like a gentleman, and all tongues in Verona bragged of him to be a virtuous and well-governed youth. Tybalt, forced to be patient against his will, restrained himself, but swore that this vile Mountague should at another time dearly pay for his intrusion.

The dancing being done, Romeo watched the place where the lady stood; and under favour of his masking habit, which might seem to excuse in part the liberty, he presumed in the gentlest manner to take her by the hand, calling it a shrine, which if he prophaned by touching it, he was a blushing pilgrim, and would kiss it for atonement. 'Good pilgrim,' answered the lady, 'your devotion shews by far too mannerly and too courtly: saints have hands, which pilgrims may touch, but kiss not.' 'Have not saints lips, and pilgrims too?' said Romeo. 'Aye,' said the lady, 'lips which they must use in prayer.' 'Oh then, my dear saint,' said Romeo, 'hear my prayer and grant it, lest I despair.' In such like allusions and loving conceits they were engaged, when the lady was called away to her mother. And Romeo enquiring who her mother was, discovered that the lady whose peerless beauty he was so much struck with, was young Juliet, daughter and heir to the lord Capulet, the great enemy of the Mountagues; and that he had unknowingly engaged his heart to his foe. This troubled him, but it could not dissuade him from loving. As little rest had Juliet, when she found that the gentleman that she had been talking with was Romeo and a Mountague, for she had been suddenly smit with the same hasty and inconsiderate passion for Romeo, which he had conceived for her; and a prodigious birth of love it seemed to her, that she must love her enemy, and that her affections should settle there, where family considerations should induce her chiefly to hate.

It being midnight, Romeo with his companions departed; but they soon missed him, for unable to stay away from the house where he had left his heart, he leaped the wall of an orchard which was at the back of Juliet's house. Here he had not been long, ruminating on his new love, when Juliet appeared above at a window, through which her exceeding beauty seemed to break like the light of the sun in the east; and the moon, which shone in the orchard with a faint light, appeared to Romeo as if sick and pale with grief at the superior lustre of this new sun. And she leaning her hand upon her cheek, he passionately wished himself a glove upon that hand, that he might touch her cheek. She all this while thinking herself alone, fetched a deep sigh, and exclaimed, 'Ah me!' Romeo, enraptured to hear her speak, said softly, and unheard by her, 'O speak again, bright angel, for such you appear, being over my head, like a winged messenger from heaven whom mortals fall back to gaze upon.' She, unconscious of being overheard, and full of the new passion which that night's adventure had given birth to, called upon her lover by name (whom she supposed absent): 'O Romeo, Romeo!' said she, 'wherefore art thou Romeo? Deny thy father, and refuse thy name, for my sake; or if thou wilt not, be but my sworn love, and I no longer will be a Capulet.' Romeo, having this encouragement, would fain have spoken, but he was desirous of hearing more; and the lady continued her passionate

Capulets Masquerade.

discourse with herself (as she thought), still chiding Romeo for being Romeo and a Mountague, and wishing him some other name, or that he would put away that hated name, and for that name, which was no part of himself, he should take all herself. At this loving word Romeo could no longer refrain, but taking up the dialogue as if her words had been addressed to him personally, and not merely in fancy, he bade her call him Love, or by whatever other name she pleased, for he was no longer Romeo, if that name was displeasing to her. Juliet, alarmed to hear a man's voice in the garden, did not at first know who it was, that by favour of the night and darkness had thus stumbled upon the discovery of her secret; but when he spoke again, though her ears had not yet drunk a hundred words of that tongue's uttering, yet so nice is a lover's hearing, that she immediately knew him to be young Romeo, and she expostulated with him on the danger to which he had exposed himself by climbing the orchard walls, for if any of her kinsmen should find him there, it would be death to him, being a Mountague. 'Alack,' said Romeo, 'there is more peril in your eye, than in twenty of their swords. Do you but look kind upon me, lady, and I am proof against their enmity. Better my life should be ended by their hate, than that hated life should be prolonged, to live without your love.' 'How came you into this place,' said Juliet, 'and by whose direction?' 'Love directed me,' answered Romeo: 'I am no pilot, yet wert thou as far apart from me, as that vast shore which is washed with the farthest sea, I should adventure for such merchandize.' A crimson blush came over Juliet's face, yet unseen by Romeo by reason of the night, when she reflected upon the discovery which she had made, yet not meaning to make it, of her love to Romeo. She would fain have recalled her words, but that was impossible: fain would she have stood upon form, and have kept her lover at a distance, as the custom of discreet ladies is, to frown and be perverse, and give their suitors harsh denials at first; to stand off, and affect a coyness or indifference, where they most love, that their lovers may not think them too lightly or too easily won: for the difficulty of attainment increases the value of the object. But there was no room in her case for denials, or puttings off, or any of the customary arts of delay and protracted courtship. Romeo had heard from her own tongue, when she did not dream that he was near her, a confession of her love. So with an honest frankness, which the novelty of her situation excused, she confirmed the truth

121

of what he had before heard, and addressing him by the name of *fair Mountague* (love can sweeten a sour name), she begged him not to impute her easy yielding to levity or an unworthy mind, but that he must lay the fault of it (if it were a fault) upon the accident of the night which had so strangely discovered her thoughts. And she added, that though her behaviour to him might not be sufficiently prudent, measured by the custom of her sex, yet that she would prove more true than many whose prudence was dissembling, and their modesty artificial cunning.

Romeo was beginning to call the heavens to witness, that nothing was farther from his thoughts than to impute a shadow of dishonour to such an honoured lady, when she stopped him, begging him not to swear; for although she joyed in him, yet she had no joy of that night's contract; it was too rash, too unadvised, too sudden. But he being urgent with her to exchange a vow of love with him that night, she said that she already had given him hers before he requested it; meaning, when he overheard her confession; but she would retract what she then bestowed, for the pleasure of giving it again, for her bounty was as infinite as the sea, and her love as deep. From this loving conference she was called away by her nurse, who slept with her, and thought it time for her to be in bed, for it was near to day-break; but hastily returning, she said three or four words more to Romeo, the purport of which was, that if his love was indeed honourable, and his purpose marriage, she would send a messenger to him to-morrow, to appoint a time for their marriage, when she would lay all her fortunes at his feet, and follow him as her lord through the world. While they were settling this point, Juliet was repeatedly called for by her nurse, and went in and returned, and went and returned again, for she seemed as jealous of Romeo going from her, as a young girl of her bird, which she will let hop a little from her hand, and pluck it back with a silken thread; and Romeo was as loth to part as she: for the sweetest music to lovers is the sound of each other's tongues at night. But at last they parted, wishing mutually sweet sleep and rest for that night.

The day was breaking when they parted, and Romeo, who was too full of thoughts of his mistress and that blessed meeting to allow him to sleep, instead of going home, bent his course to a monastery hard by, to find friar Lawrence. The good friar was already up at his devotions, but seeing young Romeo abroad so early, he conjectured rightly that he had not been a-bed that night, but that some distemper of youthful affection had kept him waking. He was right in imputing the cause of Romeo's wakefulness to love, but he made a wrong guess at the object, for he thought that his love for Rosaline had kept him waking. But when Romeo revealed his new passion for Juliet, and requested the assistance of the friar to marry them that day, the holy man lifted up his eyes and hands in a sort of wonder at the sudden change in Romeo's affections, for he had been privy to all Romeo's love for Rosaline, and his many complaints of her disdain; and he said, that young men's love lay not truly in their hearts, but in their eyes. But Romeo replying that he himself had often chidden him for doting on Rosaline, who could not love him again, whereas Juliet both loved and was beloved by him, the friar assented in some measure to his reasons; and thinking that a matrimonial alliance between young Juliet and Romeo might happily be a means of making up the long breach between the Capulets and the Mountagues; which no one more lamented than this good friar, who was a friend to both the families, and had often interposed his mediation to make up the quarrel without effect; partly moved by policy, and partly by his fondness for young Romeo, to whom he could deny nothing, the old man consented to join their hands in marriage.

Now was Romeo blest indeed, and Juliet, who knew his intent from a messenger which she had dispatched according to promise, did not fail to be early at the cell of friar Lawrence, where their hands were joined in holy marriage; the good friar praying the heavens to smile upon that act, and in the union of this young Mountague and young Capulet to bury the old strife and long dissensions of their families.

The ceremony being over, Juliet hastened home, where she staid impatient for the coming of night, at which time Romeo promised to come and meet her in the orchard, where they had met the night before; and the time between seemed as tedious to her, as the night before some great festival seems to an impatient child, that has got new finery which it may not put on till the morning.

That same day about noon, Romeo's friends, Benvolio and Mercutio, walking through the streets of Verona, were met by a party of the Capulets with the impetuous Tybalt at their head. This was the same angry Tybalt who would have fought with Romeo at

old lord Capulet's feast. He seeing Mercutio, accused him bluntly
of associating with Romeo, a Mountague. Mercutio, who had as
much fire and youthful blood in him as Tybalt, replied to this
accusation with some sharpness; and in spite of all Benvolio could
say to moderate their wrath, a quarrel was beginning, when Romeo
himself passing that way, the fierce Tybalt turned from Mercutio
to Romeo, and gave him the disgraceful appellation of villain.
Romeo wished to avoid a quarrel with Tybalt above all men,
because he was the kinsman of Juliet, and much beloved by her;
besides, this young Mountague had never thoroughly entered into
the family quarrel, being by nature wise and gentle, and the name
of a Capulet, which was his dear lady's name, was now rather a
charm to allay resentment, than a watch-word to excite fury. So
he tried to reason with Tybalt, whom he saluted mildly by the
name of *good Capulet*, as if he, though a Mountague, had some
secret pleasure in uttering that name: but Tybalt, who hated all
Mountagues as he hated hell, would hear no reason, but drew his
weapon; and Mercutio, who knew not of Romeo's secret motive for
desiring peace with Tybalt, but looked upon his present forbear-
ance as a sort of calm dishonourable submission, with many dis-
dainful words provoked Tybalt to the prosecution of his first quarrel
with him; and Tybalt and Mercutio fought, till Mercutio fell,
receiving his death's wound while Romeo and Benvolio were vainly
endeavouring to part the combatants. Mercutio being dead, Romeo
kept his temper no longer, but returned the scornful appellation of
villain which Tybalt had given him; and they fought till Tybalt
was slain by Romeo. This deadly broil falling out in the midst of
Verona at noon-day, the news of it quickly brought a crowd of
citizens to the spot, and among them the old lords Capulet and
Mountague, with their wives; and soon after arrived the prince
himself, who being related to Mercutio, whom Tybalt had slain, and
having had the peace of his government often disturbed by these
brawls of Mountagues and Capulets, came determined to put the
law in strictest force against those who should be found to be
offenders. Benvolio, who had been eye-witness to the fray, was
commanded by the prince to relate the origin of it, which he did,
keeping as near the truth as he could without injury to Romeo,
softening and excusing the part which his friends took in it. Lady
Capulet, whose extreme grief for the loss of her kinsman Tybalt
made her keep no bounds in her revenge, exhorted the prince to do

strict justice upon his murderer, and to pay no attention to Benvolio's representation, who being Romeo's friend, and a Mountague, spoke partially. Thus she pleaded against her new son-in-law, but she knew not yet that he was her son-in-law and Juliet's husband. On the other hand was to be seen Lady Mountague pleading for her child's life, and arguing with some justice that Romeo had done nothing worthy of punishment in taking the life of Tybalt, which was already forfeited to the law by his having slain Mercutio. The prince, unmoved by the passionate exclamations of these women, on a careful examination of the facts, pronounced his sentence, and by that sentence Romeo was banished from Verona.

Heavy news to young Juliet, who had been but a few hours a bride, and now by this decree seemed everlastingly divorced! When the tidings reached her, she at first gave way to rage against Romeo, who had slain her dear cousin: she called him a beautiful tyrant, a fiend angelical, a ravenous dove, a lamb with a wolf's nature, a serpent-heart hid with a flowering face, and other like contradictory names, which denoted the struggles in her mind between her love and her resentment: but in the end love got the mastery, and the tears which she shed for grief that Romeo had slain her cousin, turned to drops of joy that her husband lived whom Tybalt would have slain. Then came fresh tears, and they were altogether of grief for Romeo's banishment. That word was more terrible to her than the death of many Tybalts.

Romeo, after the fray, had taken refuge in friar Lawrence's cell, where he was first made acquainted with the prince's sentence, which seemed to him far more terrible than death. To him it appeared there was no world out of Verona's walls, no living out of the sight of Juliet. Heaven was there where Juliet lived, and all beyond was purgatory, torture, hell. The good friar would have applied the consolation of philosophy to his griefs; but this frantic young man would hear of none, but like a madman he tore his hair, and threw himself all along upon the ground, as he said, to take the measure of his grave. From this unseemly state he was roused by a message from his dear lady, which a little revived him, and then the friar took the advantage to expostulate with him on the unmanly weakness which he had shown. He had slain Tybalt, but would he also slay himself, slay his dear lady who lived but in his life? The noble form of man, he said, was but a shape of wax, when it wanted the courage which should keep it firm. The law had been lenient to him, that instead of death which he had incurred, had pronounced by the prince's mouth only banishment. He had slain Tybalt, but Tybalt would have slain him: there was a sort of happiness in that. Juliet was alive, and (beyond all hope) had become his dear wife, therein he was most happy. All these blessings, as the friar made them out to be, did Romeo put from him like a sullen misbehaved wench. And the friar bade him beware, for such as despaired (he said) died miserable. Then when Romeo was a little calmed, he counselled him that he should go that night and secretly take his leave of Juliet, and thence proceed straitways to Mantua, at which place he should sojourn, till the friar found a fit occasion to publish his marriage, which might be a joyful means of reconciling their families; and then he did not doubt but the prince would be moved to pardon him, and he would return with twenty times more joy than he went forth with grief. Romeo was convinced by these wise counsels of the friar, and took his leave to go and seek his lady, proposing to stay with her that night, and by day-break pursue his journey alone to Mantua; to which place the good friar promised to send him letters from time to time, acquainting him with the state of affairs at home.

That night Romeo passed with his dear wife, gaining secret admission to her chamber, from the orchard in which he had heard her confession of love the night before. That had been a night of unmixed joy and rapture; but the pleasures of this night, and the delight which these lovers took in each other's society, were sadly allayed with the prospect of parting, and the fatal adventures of the past day. The unwelcome day-break seemed to come too soon, and when Juliet heard the morning-song of the lark, she would have persuaded herself that it was the nightingale, which sings by night; but it was too truly the lark which sung, and a discordant and unpleasing note it seemed to her; and the streaks of day in the east too certainly pointed out that it was time for these lovers to part. Romeo took his leave of his dear wife with a heavy heart, promising to write to her from Mantua every hour in the day, and when he had descended from her chamber-window, as he stood below her on the ground, in that sad foreboding state of mind in which she was he appeared to her eyes as one dead in the bottom of a tomb. Romeo's mind misgave him in like manner; but now he

126

was forced hastily to depart, for it was death for him to be found within the walls of Verona after day-break.

This was but the beginning of the tragedy of this pair of star-crossed lovers. Romeo had not been gone many days, before the old lord Capulet proposed a match for Juliet. The husband he had chosen for her, not dreaming that she was married already, was count Paris, a gallant, young, and noble gentleman, no unworthy· suitor to the young Juliet, if she had never seen Romeo.

The terrified Juliet was in a sad perplexity at her father's offer. She pleaded her youth unsuitable to marriage, the recent death of Tybalt which had left her spirits too weak to meet a husband with any face of joy, and how indecorous it would shew for the family of the Capulets to be celebrating a nuptial-feast, when his funeral solemnities were hardly over: she pleaded every reason against the match, but the true one, namely, that she was married already. But lord Capulet was deaf to all her excuses, and in a peremptory manner ordered her to get ready, for by the following Thursday she should be married to Paris: and having found her a husband rich, young, and noble, such as the proudest maid in Verona might joyfully accept, he could not bear that out of an affected coyness, as he construed her denial, she should oppose obstacles to her own good fortune.

In this extremity Juliet applied to the friendly friar, always her counsellor in distress, and he asking her if she had resolution to undertake a desperate remedy, and she answering that she would go into the grave alive, rather than marry Paris, her own dear husband living; he directed her to go home, and appear merry, and give her consent to marry Paris, according to her father's desire, and on the next night, which was the night before the marriage, to drink of the contents of a phial which he then gave her, the effect of which would be, that for two-and-forty hours after drinking it she should appear cold and lifeless; that when the bridegroom came to fetch her in the morning, he would find her to appearance dead; that then she would be borne, as the manner in that country was, uncovered, on a bier, to be buried in the family vault; that if she could put off womanish fear, and consent to this terrible trial, in forty-two hours after swallowing the liquid (such was its certain operation) she would be sure to awake, as from a dream; and before she should awake, he would let her husband know their drift, and he should come in the night, and bear her thence to

127

Mantua. Love, and the dread of marrying Paris, gave young Juliet strength to undertake this horrible adventure; and she took the phial of the friar, promising to observe his directions.

Going from the monastery, she met the young count Paris, and, modestly dissembling, promised to become his bride. This was joyful news to the lord Capulet and his wife. It seemed to put youth into the old man: and Juliet, who had displeased him exceedingly by her refusal of the count, was his darling again, now she promised to be obedient. All things in the house were in a bustle against the approaching nuptials. No cost was spared to prepare such festival rejoicings, as Verona had never before witnessed.

On the Wednesday night Juliet drank off the potion. She had many misgivings, lest the friar, to avoid the blame which might be imputed to him for marrying her to Romeo, had given her poison; but then he was always known for a holy man: then lest she should awake before the time that Romeo was to come for her; whether the terror of the place, a vault full of dead Capulets' bones, and where Tybalt, all bloody, lay festering in his shroud, would not be enough to drive her distracted: again she thought of all the stories she had heard of spirits haunting the places where their bodies are bestowed. But then her love for Romeo, and her aversion for Paris, returned, and she desperately swallowed the draught, and became insensible.

When young Paris came early in the morning with music, to awaken his bride, instead of a living Juliet, her chamber presented the dreary spectacle of a lifeless corse. What death to his hopes! What confusion then reigned through the whole house! Poor Paris lamenting his bride, whom most detestable death had beguiled him of, had divorced from him even before their hands were joined. But still more piteous it was to hear the mournings of the old lord and lady Capulet, who having but this one, one poor loving child to rejoice and solace in, cruel death had snatched her from their sight, just as these careful parents were on the point of seeing her advanced (as they thought) by a promising and advantageous match. Now all things that were ordained for the festival, were turned from their properties to do the office of a black funeral. The wedding cheer served for a sad burial feast, the bridal hymns were changed to sullen dirges, the sprightly instruments to melancholy bells, and the flowers that should have been strewed in the bride's path, now served but to strew her corpse. Now instead of a priest to marry her, a priest was needed to bury her; and she was borne to church indeed, not to augment the cheerful hopes of the living, but to swell the dreary numbers of the dead.

Bad news, which always travels faster than good, now brought the dismal story of his Juliet's death to Romeo at Mantua, before the messenger could arrive, who was sent from friar Lawrence to apprize him that these were mock funerals only and but the shadow and representation of death, and that his dear lady lay in the tomb but for a short while, expecting when Romeo would come to release her from that dreary mansion. Just before, Romeo had been unusually joyful and light-hearted. He had dreamed in the night that he was dead (a strange dream, that gave a dead man leave to think), and that his lady came and found him dead, and breathed such life with kisses in his lips, that he revived, and was an emperor! And now that a messenger came from Verona, he thought surely it was to confirm some good news which his dreams had presaged. But when the contrary to this flattering vision appeared, and that it was his lady who was dead in truth, whom he could not revive by any kisses, he ordered horses to be got ready, for he determined that night to visit Verona, and to see his lady in her tomb. And as mischief is swift to enter into the thoughts of desperate men, he called to mind a poor apothecary, whose shop in Mantua he had lately passed, and from the beggarly appearance of the man, who seemed famished, and the wretched show in his shop of empty boxes ranged on dirty shelves, and other tokens of extreme wretchedness, he had said at the time (perhaps having some misgivings that his own disastrous life might haply meet with a conclusion so desperate), 'If a man were to need poison, which by the law of Mantua it is death to sell, here lives a poor wretch who would sell it him.' These words of his now came into his mind, and he sought out the apothecary, who, after some pretended scruples, Romeo offering him gold which his poverty could not resist, sold him a poison, which, if he swallowed, he told him, if he had the strength of twenty men, would quickly dispatch him.

With this poison he set out for Verona, to have a sight of his dear lady in her tomb, meaning, when he had satisfied his sight, to swallow the poison, and be buried by her side. He reached Verona at midnight, and found the church-yard, in the midst of which was situated the ancient tomb of the Capulets. He had provided a light, and a spade, and wrenching iron, and was proceeding to break open the monument, when he was interrupted by a voice, which by the name of *vile Mountague* bade him desist from his unlawful business. It was the young count Paris, who had come to the tomb of Juliet at that unseasonable time of night, to strew flowers and to weep over the grave of her that should have been his bride. He knew not what an interest Romeo had in the dead, but knowing him to be a Mountague, and (as he supposed) a sworn foe to all the Capulets, he judged that he was come by night to do some villanous shame to the dead bodies; therefore in an angry tone he bade him desist; and as a criminal, condemned by the laws of Verona to die if he were found within the walls of the city, he would have apprehended him. Romeo urged Paris to leave him, and warned him by the fate of Tybalt who lay buried there, not to provoke his anger, or draw down another sin upon his head, by forcing him to kill him. But the count in scorn refused his warning, and laid hands on him as a felon, which Romeo resisting, they fought, and Paris fell. When Romeo, by the help of a light, came to see who it was that he had slain, that it was Paris, who (he learned in his way from Mantua) should have married Juliet, he took the dead youth by the hand, as one whom misfortune had made a companion, and said that he would bury him in a triumphal grave, meaning in Juliet's grave, which he now opened: and there lay his lady, as one whom death had no power upon to change a feature or complexion in her matchless beauty, or as if Death were amorous, and the lean abhorred monster kept her there for his delight; for she lay yet fresh and blooming, as she had fallen to sleep when she swallowed that benumbing potion: and near her lay Tybalt in his bloody shroud, whom Romeo seeing, begged pardon of his lifeless corpse, and for Juliet's sake called him *cousin*, and said that he was about to do him a favour by putting his enemy to death. Here Romeo took his last leave of his lady's lips, kissing them; and here he shook the burden of his cross stars from his weary body, swallowing that poison which the apothecary had sold him, whose operation was fatal and real, not like that dissembling potion which Juliet had swallowed, the effect of which was now nearly expiring, and she about to awake to complain that Romeo had not kept his time, or that he had come too soon.

For now the hour was arrived at which the friar had promised that she should awake; and he, having learned that his letters which he had sent to Mantua, by some unlucky detention of the messenger, had never reached Romeo, came himself, provided with a pick-axe and lantern, to deliver the lady from her confinement; but he was surprised to find a light already burning in the Capulets' monument, and to see swords and blood near it, and Romeo and Paris lying breathless by the monument.

Before he could entertain a conjecture, to imagine how these fatal accidents had fallen out, Juliet awoke out of her trance, and seeing the friar near her, she remembered the place where she was, and the occasion of her being there, and asked for Romeo: but the friar, hearing a noise, bade her come out of that place of death, and of unnatural sleep, for a greater power than they could contradict had thwarted their intents; and being frighted by the noise of people coming, he fled; but when Juliet saw the cup closed in her true love's hands, she guessed that poison had been the cause of his end, and she would have swallowed the dregs if any had been left, and she kissed his still warm lips to try if any poison yet did hang upon them: then hearing a nearer noise of people coming, she quickly unsheathed a dagger which she wore, and stabbing herself, died by her true Romeo's side.

The watch by this time had come up to the place. A page belonging to count Paris, who had witnessed the fight between his master and Romeo, had given the alarm, which had spread among the citizens, who went up and down the streets of Verona confusedly, exclaiming, A Paris, a Romeo, a Juliet, as the rumour had imperfectly reached them, till the uproar brought lord Mountague and lord Capulet out of their beds, with the prince, to enquire into the causes of the disturbance. The friar had been apprehended by some of the watch, coming from the church-yard, trembling, sighing, and weeping, in a suspicious manner. A great multitude being assembled at the Capulets' monument, the friar was commanded by the prince to deliver what he knew of these strange and disastrous accidents.

And there, in the presence of the old lords Mountague and Capulet, he faithfully related the story of their children's fatal love, the part he took in promoting their marriage, in the hope in that union to end the long quarrels between their families; how Romeo, there dead, was husband to Juliet, and Juliet there dead, was Romeo's faithful wife: how before he could find a fit opportunity to divulge their marriage, another match was projected for Juliet, who to avoid the crime of a second marriage swallowed the sleeping draught (as he advised), and all thought her dead: how meantime he wrote to Romeo, to come and take her thence when the force of the potion should cease, and by what unfortunate miscarriage of the messenger the letters never reached Romeo: further than this the friar could not follow the story, nor knew more than that coming himself to deliver Juliet from that place of death, he found the count Paris and Romeo slain. The remainder of the transactions was supplied by the narration of the page who had seen Paris and Romeo fight, and by the servant who came with Romeo from Verona, to whom this faithful lover had given letters to be delivered to his father in the event of his death which made good the friar's words, confessing his marriage with Juliet, imploring the forgiveness of his parents, acknowledging the buying of the poison of the poor apothecary, and his intent in coming to the monument, to die, and lie with Juliet. All these circumstances agreed together to clear the friar from any hand he could be supposed to have had in these complicated slaughters, further than as the unintended consequences of his own well meant, yet too artificial and subtle contrivances.

And the prince, turning to these old lords, Mountague and Capulet, rebuked them for their brutal and irrational enmities, and shewed them what a scourge heaven had laid upon such offences, that it had found means even through the love of their children to punish their unnatural hate. And these old rivals, no longer enemies, agreed to bury their long strife in their children's graves; and lord Capulet requested lord Mountague to give him his hand, calling him by the name of brother, as if in acknowledgment of the union of their families by the marriage of the young Capulet and Mountague; and saying that lord Mountague's hand (in token of reconcilement) was all he demanded for his daughter's jointure: but lord Mountague said he would give him more, for he would raise her statue of pure gold, that while Verona kept its name, no figure should be so esteemed for its richness and workmanship as that of the true and faithful Juliet. And lord Capulet in return said that he would raise another statue to Romeo. So did these poor old lords, when it was too late, strive to outgo each other in mutual courtesies: while so deadly had been their rage and enmity in past times, that nothing but the fearful overthrow of their children (poor sacrifices to their quarrels and dissensions) could remove the rooted hates and jealousies of the noble families.

HAMLET, PRINCE OF DENMARK

Gertrude, queen of Denmark, becoming a widow by the sudden death of King Hamlet, in less than two months after his death married his brother Claudius, which was noted by all people at the time for a strange act of indiscretion, or unfeelingness, or worse: for this Claudius did no ways resemble her late husband in the qualities of his person or his mind, but was as contemptible in outward appearance, as he was base and unworthy in disposition; and suspicions did not fail to arise in the minds of some, that he had privately made away with his brother, the late king, with the view of marrying his widow, and ascending the throne of Denmark, to the exclusion of young Hamlet, the son of the buried king, and lawful successor to the throne.

But upon no one did this unadvised action of the queen make such impression as upon this young prince, who loved and venerated the memory of his dead father almost to idolatry, and being of a nice sense of honour, and a most exquisite practiser of propriety himself, did sorely take to heart this unworthy conduct of his mother Gertrude: insomuch that, between grief for his father's death and shame for his mother's marriage, this young prince was overclouded with a deep melancholy, and lost all his mirth and all his good looks; all his customary pleasure in books forsook him, his princely exercises and sports, proper to his youth, were no longer acceptable; he grew weary of the world, which seemed to him an unweeded garden, where all the wholesome flowers were choaked up, and nothing but weeds could thrive. Not that the prospect of exclusion from the throne, his lawful inheritance, weighed so much upon his spirits, though that to a young and high-minded prince was a bitter wound and a sore indignity; but what so galled him, and took away all his cheerful spirits, was, that his mother had shewn herself so forgetful to his father's memory: and such a father! who had been to her so loving and so gentle a husband! and then she always appeared as loving and obedient a wife to him, and would hang upon him as if her affection grew to him: and now within two months, or as it seemed to young Hamlet, less than two months, she had married again, married his uncle, her dead husband's brother, in itself a highly improper and

133

unlawful marriage, from the nearness of relationship, but made much more so by the indecent haste with which it was concluded, and the unkingly character of the man whom she had chosen to be the partner of her throne and bed. This it was, which, more than the loss of ten kingdoms, dashed the spirits, and brought a cloud over the mind of this honourable young prince.

In vain was all that his mother Gertrude or the king could do to contrive to divert him; he still appeared in court in a suit of deep black, as mourning for the king his father's death, which mode of dress he had never laid aside, not even in compliment to his mother upon the day she was married, nor could he be brought to join in any of the festivities or rejoicings of that (as appeared to him) disgraceful day.

What mostly troubled him was an uncertainty about the manner of his father's death. It was given out by Claudius, that a serpent had stung him: but young Hamlet had shrewd suspicions that Claudius himself was the serpent; in plain English, that he had murdered him for his crown, and that the serpent who stung his father did now sit on the throne.

How far he was right in this conjecture, and what he ought to think of his mother, how far she was privy to this murder, and whether by her consent or knowledge, or without, it came to pass, were the doubts which continually harassed and distracted him.

A rumour had reached the ear of young Hamlet, that an apparition, exactly resembling the dead king his father, had been seen by the soldiers upon watch, on the platform before the palace at midnight, for two or three nights successively. The figure came constantly clad in the same suit of armour, from head to foot, which the dead king was known to have worn: and they who saw it (Hamlet's bosom-friend Horatio was one) agreed in their testimony as to the time and manner of its appearance: that it came just as the clock struck twelve; that it looked pale, with a face more of sorrow than of anger; that its beard was grisly, and the colour a *sable silvered*, as they had seen it in his life-time: that it made no answer when they spoke to it, yet once they thought it lifted up its head, and addressed itself to motion, as if it were about to speak; but in that moment the morning cock crew, and it shrunk in haste away, and vanished out of their sight.

The young prince, strangely amazed at their relation, which was too consistent and agreeing with itself to disbelieve, concluded that it was his father's ghost which they had seen, and determined to take his watch with the soldiers that night, that he might have a chance of seeing it: for he reasoned with himself, that such an appearance did not come for nothing, but that the ghost had something to impart, and though it had been silent hitherto, yet it would speak to him. And he waited with impatience for the coming of night.

When night came he took his stand with Horatio, and Marcellus one of the guard, upon the platform, where this apparition was accustomed to walk: and it being a cold night, and the air unusually raw and nipping, Hamlet and Horatio and their companion fell into some talk about the coldness of the night, which was suddenly broken off by Horatio announcing that the ghost was coming.

At the sight of his father's spirit, Hamlet was struck with a sudden surprise and fear. He at first called upon the angels and heavenly ministers to defend them, for he knew not whether it were a good spirit or bad; whether it came for good or for evil: but he gradually assumed more courage; and his father (as it seemed to him) looked upon him so piteously, and as it were desiring to have conversation with him, and did in all respects appear so like himself as he was when he lived, that Hamlet could not help addressing him: he called him by his name, Hamlet, King, Father! and conjured him that he would tell the reason why he had left his grave, where they had seen him quietly bestowed, to come again and visit the earth and the moonlight: and besought him that he would let them know if there was any thing which they could do to give peace to his spirit. And the ghost beckoned to Hamlet, that he should go with him to some more removed place, where they might be alone: and Horatio and Marcellus would have dissuaded the young prince from following it, for they feared lest it should be some evil spirit, who would tempt him to the neighbouring sea, or to the top of some dreadful cliff, and there put on some horrible shape which might deprive the prince of his reason. But their counsels and intreaties could not alter Hamlet's determination, who cared too little about life to fear the losing of it; and as to his soul, he said, what could the spirit do to that, being a thing immortal as itself? and he felt as hardy as a lion, and bursting from them who did all they could to hold him, he followed whithersoever the spirit led him.

135

Hamlet Horatio & the Grave digger

And when they were alone together, the spirit broke silence, and told him that he was the ghost of Hamlet, his father, who had been cruelly murdered, and he told the manner of it; that it was done by his own brother Claudius, Hamlet's uncle, as Hamlet had already but too much suspected, for the hope of succeeding to his bed and crown. That as he was sleeping in his garden, his custom always in the afternoon, his treasonous brother stole upon him in his sleep, and poured the juice of poisonous henbane into his ears, which has such an antipathy to the life of man, that swift as quick-silver it courses through all the veins of the body, baking up the blood, and spreading a crust-like leprosy all over the skin: thus sleeping, by a brother's hand he was cut off at once from his crown, his queen, and his life: and he adjured Hamlet, if he did ever his dear father love, that he would revenge his foul murder. And the ghost lamented to his son, that his mother should so fall off from virtue, as to prove false to the wedded love of her first husband, and to marry his murderer: but he cautioned Hamlet, howsoever he proceeded in his revenge against his wicked uncle, by no means to act any violence against the person of his mother, but to leave her to heaven, and to the stings and thorns of conscience. And Hamlet promised to observe the ghost's direction in all things, and the ghost vanished.

And when Hamlet was left alone, he took up a solemn resolution, that all he had in his memory, all that he had ever learned by books or observation, should be instantly forgotten by him, and nothing live in his brain but the memory of what the ghost had told him, and enjoined him to do. And Hamlet related the particulars of the conversation which had passed to none but his dear friend Horatio; and he enjoined both to him and Marcellus the strictest secrecy as to what they had seen that night.

The terror which the sight of the ghost had left upon the senses of Hamlet, he being weak and dispirited before, almost unhinged his mind, and drove him beside his reason. And he, fearing that it would continue to have this effect, which might subject him to observation, and set his uncle upon his guard, if he suspected that he was meditating any thing against him, or that Hamlet really knew more of his father's death than he professed, took up a strange resolution from that time to counterfeit as if he were really and truly mad; thinking that he would be less an object of suspicion when his uncle should believe him incapable of any serious project, and that his real perturbation of mind would be best covered and pass concealed under a disguise of pretended lunacy.

From this time Hamlet affected a certain wildness and strangeness in his apparel, his speech, and behaviour, and did so excellently counterfeit the madman, that the king and queen were both deceived, and not thinking his grief for his father's death a sufficient cause to produce such a distemper, for they knew not of the appearance of the ghost, they concluded that his malady was love, and they thought they had found out the object.

Before Hamlet fell into the melancholy way which has been related, he had dearly loved a fair maid called Ophelia, the daughter of Polonius, the king's chief counsellor in affairs of state. He had sent her letters and rings, and made many tenders of his affection to her, and importuned her with love in honourable fashion: and she had given belief to his vows and importunities. But the melancholy which he fell into latterly had made him neglect her, and from the time he conceived the project of counterfeiting madness, he affected to treat her with unkindness, and a sort of rudeness; but she, good lady, rather than reproach him with being false to her, persuaded herself that it was nothing but the disease in his mind, and no settled unkindness, which had made him less observant of her than formerly; and she compared the faculties of his once noble mind and excellent understanding, impaired as they were with the deep melancholy that oppressed him, to sweet bells which in themselves are capable of most exquisite music, but when jangled out of tune, or rudely handled, produce only a harsh and unpleasing sound.

Though the rough business which Hamlet had in hand, the revenging of his father's death upon his murderer, did not suit with the playful state of courtship, or admit of the society of so idle a passion as love now seemed to him, yet it could not hinder but that soft thoughts of his Ophelia would come between, and in one of these moments, when he thought that his treatment of this gentle lady had been unreasonably harsh, he wrote her a letter full of wild starts of passion, and in extravagant terms, such as agreed with his supposed madness, but mixed with some gentle touches of affection, which could not but shew to this honoured lady that a deep love for her yet lay at the bottom of his heart. He bade her to doubt the stars were fire, and to doubt that the sun did move, to doubt truth to be a liar, but never to doubt that he loved; with more of such extravagant phrases. This letter Ophelia dutifully shewed to her father, and the old man thought himself bound to communicate it to the king and queen, who from that time supposed that the true cause of Hamlet's madness was love. And the queen wished that the good beauties of Ophelia might be the happy cause of his wildness, for so she hoped that her virtues might happily restore him to his accustomed way again, to both their honours.

But Hamlet's malady lay deeper than she supposed, or than could be so cured. His father's ghost, which he had seen, still haunted his imagination, and the sacred injunction to revenge his murder gave him no rest till it was accomplished. Every hour of delay seemed to him a sin, and a violation of his father's commands. Yet how to compass the death of the king, surrounded as he constantly was with his guards, was no easy matter. Or if it had been, the presence of the queen, Hamlet's mother, who was generally with the king, was a restraint upon his purpose, which he could not break through. Besides, the very circumstance that the usurper was his mother's husband filled him with some remorse, and still blunted the edge of his purpose. The mere act of putting a fellow-creature to death was in itself odious and terrible to a disposition naturally so gentle as Hamlet's was. His very melancholy, and the dejection of spirits he had so long been in, produced an irresoluteness and wavering of purpose, which kept him from proceeding to extremities. Moreover, he could not help having some scruples upon his mind, whether the spirit which he had seen was indeed his father, or whether it might not be the devil, who he had heard has power to take any form he pleases, and who might have assumed his father's shape only to take advantage of his weakness and his melancholy, to drive him to the doing of so desperate an act as murder. And he determined that he would have more certain grounds to go upon than a vision, or apparition, which might be a delusion.

While he was in this irresolute mind, there came to the court certain players, in whom Hamlet formerly used to take delight, and particularly to hear one of them speak a tragical speech, describing the death of old Priam, king of Troy, with the grief of Hecuba, his queen. Hamlet welcomed his old friends, the players, and remembering how that speech had formerly given him pleasure, requested the player to repeat it; which he did in so lively a manner, setting forth the cruel murder of the feeble old king, with the destruction of his people and city by fire, and the mad grief of the old queen, running barefoot up and down the palace, with a poor clout upon that head where a crown had been, and with nothing but a blanket upon her loins, snatched up in haste, where she had worn a royal robe: that not only it drew tears from all that stood by, who thought they saw the real scene, so livelily was it represented, but even the player himself delivered it with a broken voice and real tears. This put Hamlet upon thinking, if that player could so work himself up to passion by a mere fictitious speech, to weep for one that he had never seen, for Hecuba, that had been dead so many hundred years, how dull was he, who having a real motive and cue for passion, a real king and a dear father murdered, was yet so little moved, that his revenge all this while had seemed to have slept in dull and muddy forgetfulness! And while he meditated on actors and acting, and the powerful effects which a good play, represented to the life, has upon the spectator, he remembered the instance of some murderer, who seeing a murder on the stage, was by the mere force of the scene and resemblance of circumstances so affected, that on the spot he confessed the crime which he had committed. And he determined that these players should play something like the murder of his father before his uncle, and he would watch narrowly what effect it might have upon him, and from his looks he would be able to gather with more certainty if he were the murderer or not. To this effect he ordered a play to be prepared, to the representation of which he invited the king and queen.

The story of the play was of a murder done in Vienna upon a duke. The duke's name was Gonzago, his wife Baptista. The play shewed how one Lucianus, a near relation to the duke, poisoned him in his garden for his estate, and how the murderer in a short time after got the love of Gonzago's wife.

At the representation of this play the king, who did not know the trap which was laid for him, was present, with his queen and the whole court: Hamlet sitting attentively near him to observe his looks. The play began with a conversation between Gonzago and his wife, in which the lady made many protestations of love, and of never marrying a second husband, if she should outlive Gonzago; wishing she might be accursed if she ever took a second husband, and adding that no woman ever did so but those wicked women who kill their first husbands. Hamlet observed the king, his uncle, change colour at this expression, and that it was as bad as wormwood both to him and to the queen. But when Lucianus, according to the story, came to poison Gonzago sleeping in the garden, the strong resemblance which it bore to his own wicked act upon the late king, his brother, whom he had poisoned in his garden, so struck upon the conscience of this usurper, that he was unable to sit out the rest of the play, but on a sudden calling for lights to his chamber and affecting or partly feeling a sudden sickness, he abruptly left the theatre. The king being departed, the play was given over. Now Hamlet had seen enough to be satisfied that the words of the ghost were true, and no illusion; and in a fit of gaiety, like that which comes over a man who suddenly has some great doubt or scruple resolved, he swore to Horatio that he would take the ghost's word for a thousand pounds. But before he could make up his resolution as to what measures of revenge he should take, now he was certainly informed that his uncle was his father's murderer, he was sent for by the queen, his mother, to a private conference in her closet.

It was by desire of the king that the queen sent for Hamlet, that she might signify to her son how much his late behaviour had displeased them both; and the king, wishing to know all that passed at that conference, and thinking that the too partial report of a mother might let slip part of Hamlet's words, which it might much import the king to know, Polonius, the old counsellor of state, was ordered to plant himself behind the hangings in the queen's closet, where he might unseen hear all that passed. This artifice was particularly adapted to the disposition of Polonius, who was a man grown old in crooked maxims and policies of state, and delighted to get at the knowledge of matters in an indirect and cunning way.

Hamlet being come to his mother, she began to tax him in the roundest way with his actions and behaviour, and she told him that he had given great offence to *his father*, meaning the king, his uncle, whom, because he had married her, she called Hamlet's father. Hamlet, sorely indignant that she should give so dear and honoured a name as father seemed to him, to a wretch who was indeed no better than the murderer of his true father, with some sharpness replied, 'Mother, *you* have much offended *my father*.' The queen said that was but an idle answer. 'As good as the question deserved,' said Hamlet. The queen asked him if he had forgotten who it was he was speaking to? 'Alas!' replied Hamlet, 'I wish I could forget. You are the queen, your husband's brother's wife;

and you are my mother: I wish you were not what you are.' 'Nay, then,' said the queen, 'if you shew me so little respect, I will set those to you that can speak,' and was going to send the king or Polonius to him. But Hamlet would not let her go, now he had her alone, till he had tried if his words could not bring her to some sense of her wicked life; and, taking her by the wrist, he held her fast, and made her sit down. She, affrighted at his earnest manner, and fearful lest in his lunacy he should do her a mischief, cried out: and a voice was heard from behind the hangings, 'Help, help the queen;' which Hamlet hearing, and verily thinking that it was the king himself there concealed, he drew his sword, and stabbed at the place where the voice came from, as he would have stabbed a rat that ran there, till the voice ceasing, he concluded the person to be dead. But when he dragged forth the body, it was not the king, but Polonius, the old officious counsellor, that had planted himself as a spy behind the hangings. 'Oh me!' exclaimed the queen, 'what a rash and bloody deed have you done!' 'A bloody deed, mother,' replied Hamlet, 'but not so bad as yours, who killed a king, and married his brother.' Hamlet had gone too far to leave off here. He was now in the humour to speak plainly to his mother, and he pursued it. And though the faults of parents are to be tenderly treated by their children, yet in the case of great crimes the son may have leave to speak even to his own mother with some harshness, so as that harshness is meant for her good, and to turn her from her wicked ways, and not done for the purpose of upbraiding. And now this virtuous prince did in moving terms represent to the queen the heinousness of her offence, in being so forgetful of the dead king, his father, as in so short a space of time to marry with his brother and reputed murderer: such an act as, after the vows which she had sworn to her first husband, was enough to make all vows of women suspected, and all virtue to be accounted hypocrisy, wedding contracts to be less than gamesters' oaths, and religion to be a mockery and a mere form of words. He said she had done such a deed, that the heavens blushed at it, and the earth was sick of her because of it. And he shewed her two pictures, the one of the late king, her first husband, and the other of the present king, her second husband, and he bade her mark the difference: what a grace was on the brow of his father, how like a god he looked! the curls of Apollo, the forehead of Jupiter, the eye of Mars, and a posture like to Mercury newly alighted on some heaven-kissing hill! this man, he said, *had been* her husband. And then he shewed her whom she had got in his stead: how like a blight or a mildew he looked, for so he had blasted his wholesome brother. And the queen was sore ashamed that he should so turn her eyes inward upon her soul, which she now saw so black and deformed. And he asked her how she could continue to live with this man, and be a wife to him, who had murdered her first husband, and got the crown by as false means as a thief — And just as he spoke, the ghost of his father, such as he was in his life-time, and such as he had lately seen it, entered the room, and Hamlet, in great terror, asked what it would have; and the ghost said that it came to remind him of the revenge he had promised, which Hamlet seemed to have forgot: and the ghost bade him speak to his mother, for the grief and terror she was in would else kill her. It then vanished, and was seen by none but Hamlet, neither could he by pointing to where it stood, or by any description, make his mother perceive it; who was terribly frighted all this while to hear him conversing, as it seemed to her, with nothing: and she imputed it to the disorder of his mind. But Hamlet begged her not to flatter her wicked soul in such a manner as to think that it was his madness, and not her own offences, which had brought his father's spirit again on the earth. And he bade her feel his pulse, how temperately it beat, not like a madman's. And he begged of her with tears, to confess herself to heaven for what was past, and for the future to avoid the company of the king, and be no more as a wife to him: and when she should shew herself a mother to him, by respecting his father's memory, he would ask a blessing of her as a son. And she promising to observe his directions, the conference ended.

And now Hamlet was at leisure to consider who it was that in his unfortunate rashness he had killed: and when he came to see that it was Polonius, the father of the lady Ophelia, whom he so dearly loved, he drew apart the dead body, and, his spirits being now a little quieter, he wept for what he had done.

The unfortunate death of Polonius gave the king a pretence for sending Hamlet out of the kingdom. He would willingly have put him to death, fearing him as dangerous; but he dreaded the people, who loved Hamlet; and the queen, who, with all her faults, doted upon the prince, her son. So this subtle king, under pretence of providing for Hamlet's safety, that he might not be called to account for Polonius' death, caused him to be conveyed on board a ship bound for England, under the care of two courtiers, by whom he dispatched letters to the English court, which at that time was in subjection and paid tribute to Denmark, requiring for special reasons there pretended, that Hamlet should be put to death as soon as he landed on English ground. Hamlet, suspecting some treachery, in the night-time secretly got at the letters, and skilfully erasing his own name, he in the stead of it put in the names of those two courtiers, who had the charge of him, to be put to death: then sealing up the letters, he put them into their place again. Soon after the ship was attacked by pirates, and a sea-fight commenced; in the course of which Hamlet, desirous to shew his valour, with sword in hand singly boarded the enemy's vessel; while his own ship, in a cowardly manner, bore away, and leaving him to his fate, the two courtiers made the best of their way to England, charged with those letters the sense of which Hamlet had altered to their own deserved destruction.

The pirates, who had the prince in their power, shewed themselves gentle enemies; and knowing whom they had got prisoner, in the hope that the prince might do them a good turn at court in recompence for any favour they might shew him, they set Hamlet on shore at the nearest port in Denmark. From that place Hamlet wrote to the king, acquainting him with the strange chance which had brought him back to his own country, and saying that on the next day he should present himself before his majesty. When he got home, a sad spectacle offered itself the first thing to his eyes.

This was the funeral of the young and beautiful Ophelia, his once dear mistress. The wits of this young lady had begun to turn ever since her poor father's death. That he should die a violent death, and by the hands of the prince whom she loved, so affected this tender young maid, that in a little time she grew perfectly distracted, and would go about giving flowers away to the ladies of the court, and saying that they were for her father's burial, singing songs about love and about death, and sometimes such as had no meaning at all, as if she had no memory of what had happened to her. There was a willow which grew slanting over a brook, and reflected its leaves in the stream. To this brook she came one day when she was unwatched, with garlands she had been making, mixed up of daisies and nettles, flowers and weeds together, and clambering up to hang her garland upon the boughs of the willow, a bow broke and precipitated this fair young maid, garland, and all that she had gathered, into the water, where her clothes bore her up for a while, during which she chaunted scraps of old tunes, like one insensible to her own distress, or as if she were a creature natural to that element: but long it was not before her garments, heavy with the wet, pulled her in from her melodious singing to a muddy and miserable death. It was the funeral of this fair maid which her brother Laertes was celebrating, the king and queen and whole court being present, when Hamlet arrived. He knew not what all this shew imported, but stood on one side, not inclining to interrupt the ceremony. He saw the flowers strewed upon her grave, as the custom was in maiden burials, which the queen herself threw in; and as she threw them, she said, 'Sweets to the sweet! I thought to have decked thy bride-bed, sweet maid, not to have strewed thy grave. Thou shouldst have been my Hamlet's wife.' And he heard her brother wish that violets might spring from her grave: and he saw him leap into the grave all frantic with grief, and bid the attendants pile mountains of earth upon him, that he might be buried with her. And Hamlet's love for this fair maid came back to him, and he could not bear that a brother should shew so much transport of grief, for he thought that he loved Ophelia better than forty thousand brothers. Then discovering himself, he leaped into the grave where Laertes was, all as frantic or more frantic than he, and Laertes knowing him to be Hamlet, who had been the cause of his father's and his sister's death, grappled him by the throat as an enemy, till the attendants parted them: and Hamlet, after the funeral, excused his hasty act in throwing himself into the grave as if to brave Laertes; but he said he could not bear that any one should seem to outgo him in grief for the death of the fair Ophelia. And for the time these two noble youths seemed reconciled.

But out of the grief and anger of Laertes for the death of his father and Ophelia, the king, Hamlet's wicked uncle, contrived destruction for Hamlet. He set on Laertes, under cover of peace and reconciliation, to challenge Hamlet to a friendly trial of skill at fencing, which Hamlet accepting, a day was appointed to try the match. At this match all the court was present, and Laertes, by direction of the king, prepared a poisoned weapon. Upon this match great wagers were laid by the courtiers, as both Hamlet and Laertes were known to excel at this sword-play; and Hamlet taking up the foils chose one, not at all suspecting the treachery of Laertes, or being careful to examine Laertes' weapon, who, instead of a foil or blunted sword, which the laws of fencing require, made use of one with a point, and poisoned. At first Laertes did but play with Hamlet, and suffered him to gain some advantages, which the dissembling king magnified and extolled beyond measure, drinking to Hamlet's success, and wagering rich bets upon the issue: but after a few passes, Laertes growing warm made a deadly thrust at Hamlet with his poisoned weapon, and gave him a mortal blow. Hamlet incensed, but not knowing the whole of the treachery, in the scuffle exchanged his own innocent weapon for Laertes' deadly one, and with a thrust of Laertes' own sword repaid Laertes home, who was thus justly caught in his own treachery. In this instant the queen shrieked out that she was poisoned. She had inadvertently drunk out of a bowl which the king had prepared for Hamlet, in case that being warm in fencing he should call for drink: into this the treacherous king had infused a deadly poison, to make sure of Hamlet, if Laertes had failed. He had forgotten to warn the queen of the bowl, which she drank of, and immediately died, exclaiming with her last breath that she was poisoned. Hamlet, suspecting some treachery, ordered the doors to be shut, while he sought it out. Laertes told him to seek no further, for he was the traitor; and feeling his life go away with the wound which Hamlet had given him, he made confession of the treachery he had used, and how he had fallen a victim to it: and he told Hamlet of the envenomed point, and said that Hamlet had not half an hour to live, for no medicine could cure him; and begging forgiveness of Hamlet he died, with his last words accusing the king of being the contriver of the mischief. When Hamlet saw his end draw near, there being yet some venom left upon the sword, he suddenly turned upon his false uncle, and thrust the point of it to his heart, fulfilling the promise which he had made to his father's spirit, whose injunction was now accomplished, and his foul murder revenged upon the murderer. Then Hamlet, feeling his breath fail and life departing, turned to his dear friend Horatio, who had been spectator of this fatal tragedy; and with his dying breath requested him that he would live to tell his story to the world (for Horatio had made a motion as if he would slay himself to accompany the prince in death), and Horatio promised that he would make a true report, as one that was privy to all the circumstances. And, thus satisfied, the noble heart of Hamlet cracked: and Horatio and the by-standers with many tears commended the spirit of their sweet prince to the guardianship of angels. For Hamlet was a loving and a gentle prince, and greatly beloved for his many noble and prince-like qualities; and if he had lived, would no doubt have proved a most royal and complete king to Denmark.

OTHELLO

Brabantio, the rich senator of Venice, had a fair daughter, the gentle Desdemona. She was sought to by divers suitors, both on account of her many virtuous qualities and for her rich expectations. But among the suitors of her own clime and complexion she saw none whom she could affect: for this noble lady, who regarded the mind more than the features of men, with a singularity rather to be admired than imitated, had chosen for the object of her affections a Moor, a black, whom her father loved, and often invited to his house.

Neither is Desdemona to be altogether condemned for the un-suitableness of the person whom she selected for her lover. Bating that Othello was black, the noble Moor wanted nothing which might recommend him to the affections of the greatest lady. He was a soldier, and a brave one; and by his conduct in bloody wars against the Turks, had risen to the rank of general in the Venetian service, and was esteemed and trusted by the state.

He had been a traveller, and Desdemona (as is the manner of ladies) loved to hear him tell the story of his adventures, which he would run through from his earliest recollection; the battles, sieges, and encounters, which he had past through; the perils he had been exposed to by land and by water; his hair-breadth escapes, when he has entered a breach, or marched up to the mouth of a cannon; and how he had been taken prisoner by the insolent enemy, and sold to slavery: how he demeaned himself in that state, and how he escaped: all these accounts, added to the narration of the strange things he had seen in foreign countries, the vast wilder-nesses and romantic caverns, the quarries, the rocks and mountains, whose heads are in the clouds; of the savage nations, the cannibals who are man-eaters, and a race of people in Africa whose heads do grow beneath their shoulders: these travellers' stories would so enchain the attention of Desdemona, that if she were called off at any time by household affairs, she would dispatch with all haste that business, and return, and with a greedy ear devour Othello's discourse. And once he took advantage of a pliant hour, and drew from her a prayer, that he would tell her the whole story of his life at large, of which she had heard so much, but only by parts: to which he consented, and beguiled her of many a tear, when he spoke of some distressful stroke which his youth suffered.

His story being done, she gave him for his pains a world of sighs: she swore a pretty oath, that it was all passing strange, and pitiful, wondrous pitiful: she wished (she said) she had not heard it, yet she wished that heaven had made her such a man: and then she thanked him, and told him, if he had a friend who loved her, he had only to teach him how to tell his story, and that would woo her. Upon this hint, delivered not with more frankness than modesty, accompanied with a certain bewitching prettiness, and blushes, which Othello could not but understand, he spoke more openly of his love, and in this golden opportunity gained the consent of the generous lady Desdemona privately to marry him.

Neither Othello's colour nor his fortune were such, that it could be hoped Brabantio would accept him for a son-in-law. He had left his daughter free; but he did expect that, as the manner of noble Venetian ladies was, she would choose ere long a husband of senatorial rank or expectations: but in this he was deceived; Desdemona loved the Moor, though he was black, and devoted her heart and fortunes to his valiant parts and qualities: so was her heart subdued to an implicit devotion to the man she had selected for a husband, that his very colour, which to all but this discerning lady would have proved an insurmountable objection, was by her esteemed above all the white skins and clear complexions of the young Venetian nobility, her suitors.

Their marriage, which, though privately carried, could not long be kept a secret, came to the ears of the old man, Brabantio, who appeared in a solemn council of the senate, as an accuser of the Moor Othello, who by spells and witchcraft (he maintained) had seduced the affections of the fair Desdemona to marry him, without the consent of her father, and against the obligations of hospitality.

At this juncture of time it happened that the state of Venice had immediate need of the services of Othello, news having arrived that the Turks with mighty preparation had fitted out a fleet, which was bending its course to the island of Cyprus, with intent to regain that strong post from the Venetians, who then held it: in this emergency the state turned its eyes upon Othello, who alone was deemed adequate to conduct the defence of Cyprus against the Turks. So that Othello, now summoned before the senate, stood in their presence at once as a candidate for a great state-employment, and as a culprit, charged with offences which by the laws of Venice were made capital.

The age and senatorial character of old Brabantio commanded a most patient hearing from that grave assembly; but the incensed father conducted his accusation with so much intemperance, producing likelihoods and allegations for proofs, that, when Othello was called upon for his defence, he had only to relate a plain tale of the course of his love; which he did with such an artless eloquence, recounting the whole story of his wooing, as we have related it above, and delivered his speech with so noble a plainness (the evidence of truth), that the duke, who sat as chief judge, could not help confessing, that a tale so told would have won his daughter too: and the spells and conjurations, which Othello had used in his courtship, plainly appeared to have been no more than the honest arts of men in love; and the only witchcraft which he had used the faculty of telling a soft tale to win a lady's ear.

This statement of Othello was confirmed by the testimony of the lady Desdemona herself, who appeared in court, and professing a duty to her father for life and education, challenged leave of him to profess a yet higher duty to her lord and husband, even so much as her mother had shewn in preferring him (Brabantio) above *her* father.

The old senator, unable to maintain his plea, called the Moor to him with many expressions of sorrow, and, as an act of necessity, bestowed upon him his daughter, whom, if he had been free to withhold her, (he told him) he would with all his heart have kept from him; adding, that he was glad at soul that he had no other child, for this behaviour of Desdemona would have taught him to be a tyrant, and hang clogs on them for her desertion.

This difficulty being got over, Othello, to whom custom had rendered the hardships of a military life as natural as food and rest are to other men, readily undertook the management of the wars in Cyprus: and Desdemona, preferring the honour of her lord (though with danger) before the indulgence of those idle delights in which new-married people usually waste their time, cheerfully consented to his going.

No sooner were Othello and his lady landed in Cyprus, than news arrived, that a desperate tempest had dispersed the Turkish fleet, and thus the island was secure from any immediate apprehension of an attack. But the war, which Othello was to suffer, was now beginning: and the enemies, which malice stirred up against his innocent lady, proved in their nature more deadly than strangers or infidels.

Among all the general's friends no one possessed the confidence of Othello more entirely than Cassio. Michael Cassio was a young soldier, a Florentine, gay, amorous, and of pleasing address, favourite qualities with women; he was handsome, and eloquent, and exactly such a person as might alarm the jealousy of a man advanced in years (as Othello in some measure was), who had married a young and beautiful wife; but Othello was as free from jealousy as he was noble, and as incapable of suspecting, as of doing, a base action. He had employed this Cassio in his love-affair with Desdemona, and Cassio had been a sort of go-between in his suit: for Othello, fearing that himself had not those soft parts of conversation which please ladies, and finding these qualities in his friend, would often depute Cassio to go (as he phrased it) a courting for him: such innocent simplicity being rather an honour than a blemish to the character of the valiant Moor. So that no wonder, if next to Othello himself (but at far distance, as beseems a virtuous wife) the gentle Desdemona loved and trusted Cassio. Nor had the marriage of this couple made any difference in their behaviour to Michael Cassio. He frequented their house, and his free and rattling talk was no unpleasing variety to Othello, who was himself of a more serious temper: for such tempers are observed often to delight in their contraries, as a relief from the oppressive excess of their own: and Desdemona and Cassio would talk and laugh together, as in the days when he went a courting for his friend.

Othello had lately promoted Cassio to be the lieutenant, a place of trust, and nearest to the general's person. This promotion gave great offence to Iago, an older officer, who thought he had a better claim than Cassio, and would often ridicule Cassio, as a fellow fit only for the company of ladies, and one that knew no more of the art of war, or how to set an army in array for battle, than a girl.

150

Iago hated Cassio, and he hated Othello, as well for favouring Cassio, as for an unjust suspicion, which he had lightly taken up against Othello, that the Moor was too fond of Iago's wife Emilia. From these imaginary provocations, the plotting mind of Iago conceived a horrid scheme of revenge, which should involve both Cassio, the Moor, and Desdemona in one common ruin.

Iago was artful, and had studied human nature deeply, and he knew that of all the torments which afflict the mind of man (and far beyond bodily torture), the pains of jealousy were the most intolerable, and had the sorest sting. If he could succeed in making Othello jealous of Cassio, he thought it would be an exquisite plot of revenge, and might end in the death of Cassio or Othello, or both; he cared not.

The arrival of the general and his lady in Cyprus, meeting with the news of the dispersion of the enemy's fleet, made a sort of holiday in the island. Every body gave themselves up to feasting and making merry. Wine flowed in abundance, and cups went round to the health of the black Othello, and his lady the fair Desdemona.

Cassio had the direction of the guard that night, with a charge from Othello to keep the soldiers from excess in drinking, that no brawl might arise, to fright the inhabitants, or disgust them with the new-landed forces. That night Iago began his deep-laid plans of mischief; under cover of loyalty and love to the general, he enticed Cassio to make rather too free with the bottle (a great fault in an officer upon guard). Cassio for a time resisted, but he could not long hold out against the honest freedom which Iago knew how to put on, but kept swallowing glass after glass (as Iago still plied him with drink and encouraging songs), and Cassio's tongue ran over in praise of the lady Desdemona, whom he again and again toasted, affirming that she was a most exquisite lady: until at last the enemy which he put into his mouth, stole away his brains; and upon some provocation given him by a fellow whom Iago had set on, swords were drawn, and Montano, a worthy officer, who interfered to appease the dispute, was wounded in the scuffle. The riot now began to be general, and Iago, who had set on foot the mischief, was foremost in spreading the alarm, causing the castle-bell to be rung (as if some dangerous mutiny instead of a slight drunken quarrel had arisen): the alarm-bell ringing awakened Othello, who, dressing in a hurry, and coming to the scene of action, questioned

Othello preparing to kill his Wife.

Cassio of the cause. Cassio was now come to himself, the effect of the wine having a little gone off, but was too much ashamed to reply; and Iago, pretending a great reluctance to accuse Cassio, but as it were forced into it by Othello, who insisted to know the truth, gave an account of the whole matter (leaving out his own share in it, which Cassio was too far gone to remember) in such a manner, as while he seemed to make Cassio's offence less, did indeed make it appear greater than it was. The result was, that Othello, who was a strict observer of discipline, was compelled to take away Cassio's place of lieutenant from him.

Thus did Iago's first artifice succeed completely; he had now undermined his hated rival, and thrust him out of his place: but a further use was hereafter to be made of the adventure of this disastrous night.

Cassio, whom this misfortune had entirely sobered, now lamented to his seeming friend Iago that he should have been such a fool as to transform himself into a beast. He was undone, for how could he ask the general for his place again! he would tell him he was a drunkard. He despised himself. Iago, affecting to make light of it, said, that he, or any man living, might be drunk upon occasion; it remained now to make the best of a bad bargain; the general's wife was now the general, and could do any thing with Othello; that he were best to apply to the lady Desdemona to mediate for him with her lord; that she was of a frank, obliging disposition, and would readily undertake a good office of this sort, and set Cassio right again in the general's favour; and then this crack in their love would be made stronger than ever. A good advice of Iago, if it had not been given for wicked purposes, which will after appear.

Cassio did as Iago advised him, and made application to the lady Desdemona, who was easy to be won over in any honest suit; and she promised Cassio that she would be his solicitor with her lord, and rather die than give up his cause. This she immediately set about in so earnest and pretty a manner, that Othello, who was mortally offended with Cassio, could not put her off. When he pleaded delay, and that it was too soon to pardon such an offender, she would not be beat back, but insisted that it should be the next night, or the morning after, or the next morning to that at farthest. Then she shewed how penitent and humbled poor Cassio was, and that his offence did not deserve so sharp a check. And when Othello still hung back, 'What! my lord,' said she, 'that I should have so

much to do to plead for Cassio, Michael Cassio, that came a courting for you, and oftentimes, when I have spoken in dispraise of
you, has taken your part! I count this but a little thing to ask of
you. When I mean to try your love indeed, I shall ask a weighty
matter.' Othello could deny nothing to such a pleader, and only
requesting that Desdemona would leave the time to him, promised
to receive Michael Cassio again into favour.

It happened that Othello and Iago had entered into the room
where Desdemona was, just as Cassio, who had been imploring her
intercession, was departing at the opposite door; and Iago, who was
full of art, said in a low voice, as if to himself, 'I like not that.'
Othello took no great notice of what he said; indeed the conference
which immediately took place with his lady put it out of his head;
but he remembered it afterwards. For when Desdemona was gone,
Iago, as if for mere satisfaction of his thought, questioned Othello
whether Michael Cassio, when Othello was courting his lady, knew
of his love. To this the general answering in the affirmative, and
adding, that he had gone between them very often during the
courtship, Iago knitted his brow, as if he had got fresh light of some
terrible matter, and cried, 'Indeed!' This brought into Othello's
mind the words which Iago had let fall upon entering the room
and seeing Cassio with Desdemona; and he began to think there
was some meaning in all this: for he deemed Iago to be a just man,
and full of love and honesty, and what in a false knave would be
tricks, in him seemed to be the natural workings of an honest mind,
big with something too great for utterance: and Othello prayed
Iago to speak what he knew, and to give his worst thoughts words.
'And what,' said Iago, 'if some thoughts very vile should have
intruded into my breast, as where is the palace into which foul
things do not enter?' Then Iago went on to say, what a pity it
were, if any trouble should arise to Othello out of his imperfect
observations; that it would not be for Othello's peace to know
his thoughts; that people's good names were not to be taken away
for slight suspicions; and when Othello's curiosity was raised
almost to distraction with these hints and scattered words, Iago, as
if in earnest care for Othello's peace of mind, besought him to
beware of jealousy: with such art did this villain raise suspicions
in the unguarded Othello, by the very caution which he pretended
to give him against suspicion. 'I know,' said Othello, 'that my wife
is fair, loves company and feasting, is free of speech, sings, plays,

and dances well: but where virtue is, these qualities are virtuous. I must have proof before I think her dishonest.' Then Iago, as if glad that Othello was slow to believe ill of his lady, frankly declared that he had no proof, but begged Othello to observe her behaviour well, when Cassio was by; not to be jealous, nor too secure neither, for that he (Iago) knew the dispositions of the Italian ladies, his country-women, better than Othello could do; and that in Venice the wives let heaven see many pranks they dared not shew their husbands. Then he artfully insinuated, that Desdemona deceived her father in marrying with Othello, and carried it so closely, that the poor old man thought that witchcraft had been used. Othello was much moved with this argument, which brought the matter home to him, for if she had deceived her father, why might she not deceive her husband?

Iago begged pardon for having moved him but Othello, assuming an indifference, while he was really shaken with inward grief at Iago's words, begged him to go on, which Iago did with many apologies, as if unwilling to produce any thing against Cassio, whom he called his friend: he then came strongly to the point, and reminded Othello how Desdemona had refused many suitable matches of her own clime and complexion, and had married him, a Moor, which shewed unnatural in her, and proved her to have a headstrong will: and when her better judgment returned, how probable it was she should fall upon comparing Othello with the fine forms and clear white complexions of the young Italians her countrymen. He concluded with advising Othello to put off his reconcilement with Cassio a little longer, and in the mean while to note with what earnestness Desdemona should intercede in his behalf; for that much would be seen in that. So mischievously did this artful villain lay his plots to turn the gentle qualities of this innocent lady into her destruction, and make a net for her out of her own goodness to entrap her: first setting Cassio on to intreat her mediation, and then out of that very mediation contriving stratagems for her ruin.

The conference ended with Iago's begging Othello to account his wife innocent, until he had more decisive proof; and Othello promised to be patient: but from that moment the deceived Othello never tasted content of mind. Poppy, nor the juice of mandragora, nor all the sleeping potions in the world, could ever again restore to him that sweet rest, which he had enjoyed but yesterday. His occupation sickened upon him. He no longer took delight in arms. His heart, that used to be roused at the sight of troops, and banners, and battle-array, and would stir and leap at the sound of a drum, or a trumpet, or a neighing warhorse, seemed to have lost all that pride and ambition, which are a soldier's virtue; and his military ardour and all his old joys forsook him. Sometimes he thought his wife honest, and at times he thought her not so; sometimes he thought Iago just, and at times he thought him not so; then he would wish that he had never known of it; he was not the worse for her loving Cassio, so long as he knew it not: torn in pieces with these distracting thoughts, he once laid hold on Iago's throat, and demanded proof of Desdemona's guilt, or threatened instant death for his having belied her. Iago, feigning indignation that his honesty should be taken for a vice, asked Othello, if he had not sometimes seen a handkerchief spotted with strawberries in his wife's hand. Othello answered, that he had given her such a one, and that it was his first gift. 'That same handkerchief,' said Iago, 'did I see Michael Cassio this day wipe his face with.' 'If it be as you say,' said Othello, 'I will not rest till a wide revenge swallow them up: and first, for a token of your fidelity, I expect that Cassio shall be put to death within three days; and for that fair devil [meaning his lady], I will withdraw and devise some swift means of death for her.'

Trifles, light as air, are to the jealous proofs as strong as holy writ. A handkerchief of his wife's seen in Cassio's hand, was motive enough to the deluded Othello to pass sentence of death upon them both, without once enquiring how Cassio came by it. Desdemona had never given such a present to Cassio, nor would this constant lady have wronged her lord with doing so naughty a thing, as giving his presents to another man; both Cassio and Desdemona were innocent of any offence aginst Othello: but the wicked Iago, whose spirits never slept in contrivance of villainy, had made his wife (a good, but a weak woman) steal this handkerchief from Desdemona, under pretence of getting the work copied, but in reality to drop it in Cassio's way, where he might find it, and give a handle to Iago's suggestion that it was Desdemona's present.

Othello, soon after meeting his wife, pretended that he had a head-ache (as he might indeed with truth), and desired her to lend him her handkerchief to hold to his temples. She did so. 'Not this,' said Othello, 'but that handkerchief I gave you.' Desdemona had it not about her (for indeed it was stolen as we have related). 'How! ' said Othello, 'this is a fault indeed. That handkerchief an Egyptian woman gave to my mother; the woman was a witch, and could read people's thoughts; she told my mother, while she kept it, it would make her amiable, and my father would love her; but, if she lost it, or gave it away, my father's fancy would turn, and he would lothe her as much as he had loved. her. She dying gave it me, and bade me, if I ever married, to give it to my wife. I did so; take heed of it. Make it a darling as precious as your eye.' 'Is it possible?' said the frighted lady. 'Tis true: ' continued Othello; 'it is a magical handkerchief; a sibyl that had lived in the world two hundred years, in a fit of prophetic fury worked it; the silk-worms that furnished the silk were hallowed, and it was dyed in mummy of maidens' hearts conserved.' Desdemona, hearing the wondrous virtues of the handkerchief, was ready to die with fear, for she plainly perceived she had lost it, and with it, she feared, the affections of her husband. Then Othello started, and looked as if he were going to do some rash thing, and still he demanded the handkerchief, which when she could not produce, she tried to divert her husband from too serious thoughts, and cheerfully told him, she saw all his talk about the handkerchief was only to put her off from her suit about Michael Cassio, whom she went on to praise (as Iago had foretold), till Othello in perfect distraction burst out of the room, and then Desdemona, though unwillingly, began to suspect her lord was jealous.

What cause she could have ministered to him she knew not, and then she accused herself for accusing the noble Othello, and thought to be sure that some untoward news from Venice, or some state troubles, had puddled his spirits, and made his temper not so sweet as formerly. And she said, 'Men are not gods, and we must not look for that observance from them when they are married, which they shew us on the bridal day.' And she beshrewed herself for so unkindly judging of his unkindness.

Again Othello and Desdemona met, and he accused her more plainly of being unfaithful, and of loving another man, but he did not name whom: and Othello wept, and Desdemona said, 'Alas! the heavy day! why do you weep?' And Othello told her, he could have borne all sorts of evils with fortitude – poverty, and disease, and disgrace; but her infidelity had broken his heart: and he called her a weed, that looked so fair, and smelled so sweet, that the sense

157

ached at it; and wished she had never been born. And when he had left her, this innocent lady was so stupefied with wonder at her lord's untrue suspicion of her, that a weightlike sleep came over her, and she only desired her attendant to make her bed, and to lay her wedding-sheets upon it, saying, that when people teach their babes, they do it by gentle means and easy tasks, and Othello might have chid her so; for in good faith she was a child when she was chidden. And this was all the complaint which this gentle lady made.

Desdemona being retired to bed expecting her lord would follow her, soon fell into a slumber the effect of her troubled spirits, when Othello entered the chamber, full of the black purpose which he had meditated of putting his lady to death. But when he saw her asleep, he thought he would not shed her blood, nor scar that white skin of hers, more white than alabaster. But he was resolved she should die; else (as he said) she would live to betray more men, as she had done him. Then he kissed her for the last time (as he said), and that kiss was so sweet, he must needs kiss her again: and he wept, but he said they were cruel tears.

Desdemona was awakened with his kisses, and she looked upon Othello, and she saw him gnaw his under-lip, and roll his eyes, and she knew he was always fatal when he looked so: and he bade her prepare for death, and to say her prayers, for he would not kill her soul. And this innocent wife, as she lay at his mercy, begged for compassion, and to know her fault, and then he named Cassio, and the handkerchief which (he said) she had given him; and as the guiltless lady was proceeding to clear herself, he suddenly would hear no more, but covering her up in the bed-clothes, stifled her till she died.

In this instant of time was brought into the house Cassio, wounded and bleeding, whom Iago had set one of his creatures on to assassinate; but the fellow not succeeding in his attempt to kill Cassio (whom he wounded, but not mortally), and being himself killed by Iago to prevent discovery, in his pockets were found certain letters, which made the guilt of Iago, and the innocence of Cassio, clear beyond all doubt; and Cassio now came to beg pardon of Othello, and to ask wherein he had offended him, that he had employed Iago to murder him.

This discovery was as a thunderstroke to Othello, who now plainly saw that he was no better than a murderer, and that his wife (poor innocent lady) had been ever faithful to him; the extreme anguish of which discovery making life insupportable, he fell upon his sword, and throwing himself upon the body of his dear injured lady, expired.

These rash acts raised much passion of horror and amazement in the by-standers, for Othello had borne a fair reputation, and till he was wrought upon by the arts of a villain, which his own noble nature never gave him leave to suspect, he was a loving and a doting husband. He had loved, not wisely, but too well; and his manly eyes (when he learned his mistake), though not used to weep on every small occasion, dropt tears as fast as the Arabian trees their gum. And when he was dead all his former merits and his valiant acts were remembered. Nothing now remained for his successor, but to put the utmost censure of the law in force against Iago, who was executed with strict tortures; and to send word to the state of Venice of the lamentable death of their renowned general.

NOTES

Introduction

1 *Coleridge's Miscellaneous Criticism*, ed. T. M. Raysor (London: Constable, 1936), p. 412.

2 'Characters of Shakespear's Plays', *Complete Works*, ed. P. P. Howe (London: J. M. Dent, 1930) IV, 270.

3 Barry Cornwall, *Charles Lamb* (Boston: Roberts Brothers, 1866), p. 23.

4 'Drury Lane Theatre. Richard Duke of York', *The Champion*, 28 December, 1817.

5 *Letters*, I, 273.

6 Lamb's father worked as a kind of private secretary to Samuel Salt, M.P., a wealthy bencher of the Inner Temple. Salt took an active interest in the education of the Lamb children and made his own extensive library open to them.

7 'Detached Thoughts on Books and Reading', *The Last Essays of Elia* (*Works*, II, 173).

8 *Letters*, I, 159.

9 All quotations in this paragraph are from 'On the Tragedies of Shakspeare', *Works*, I, 97-111.

10 *The Letters of Charles Lamb*, ed. E. V. Lucas (London: Dent and Methuen, 1935), III, 82.

11 'The Nineteenth Century', *Cambridge History of English Literature* (Cambridge University Press, 1961), XII, 189.

12 *Oxford Lectures on Poetry* (London: Macmillan, 1909), p. 105.

13 John Dover Wilson, ed. *Richard III* (Cambridge University Press, 1954), xxxvii.

14 E. V. Lucas, *The Life of Charles Lamb* (London: Methuen, 1905), p. 469.

Part I

1 Leigh Hunt thought Cooke an excellent Richard but he confirms the details of Lamb's description: 'Much of this character is occupied by the display of a confident dissimulation, which is something very different from the dignity of tragedy. . . . His shrinking rise of the shoulders . . . gave an idea of that contracted watchfulness, with which a mean hypocrite retires into himself . . . his sarcastic cast of counten-

ance with its close wideness of smile and its hooked nose. . . . Mr Cooke is the Machiavel of the modern stage.' *Critical Essays on the Performers of the London Theatres* (London, 1807), pp. 216-222.

2 Demosthenes (c. 383-322 B.C.) and Edmund Burke (1729-1797) represented for Lamb the greatest orators of ancient Greek and recent English history respectively.

3 James Quin (1693-1766), who performed at the Drury Lane Theatre from 1714-1751, was eclipsed by David Garrick (1717-1779). One of Britain's most versatile actors, Garrick made his formal London debut in 1742 as Richard III. Spranger Barry (1719-1777) alternated leading roles with Garrick at Drury Lane until in 1750 he moved to Covent Garden, where he attempted to rival Garrick in the parts of Richard III and Hamlet.

4 A line added to the play by Cibber. It was so well known as a theatrical 'point' that it was maintained in productions long after Shakespeare's own text had been restored to the stage.

5 A misquotation of one of Cibber's own lines: 'But I've a Tongue shall wheadle with the Devil', II. i. 61.

6 Lamb is footnoting an extract from Robert Davenport's play *King John and Matilda* (c. 1631).

7 Shakespeare's lines read:

> And therefore, since I cannot prove a lover
> To entertain these fair well-spoken days,
> I am determined to prove a villain.

(I. i. 28-30)

8 The first entry under 'villain' in the *Oxford English Dictionary* is 'Deficient in courtesy or good-breeding; boorish, clownish. Obs.'

9 *I Henry IV*, I. iii. 209.

10 *Richard III*, I. iv. 1-75.

11 *The Winter's Tale*, III. iii. 15-46.

12 'The things that day most minds, at night doe most appeare.' *Faerie Queene*, IV. v. 43.

Part II

1 Westminster Abbey, London, where David Garrick was buried.

2 The lines on Garrick's monument were by Samuel Jackson Pratt (1749-1814), of whom Lamb wrote elsewhere: 'The gentleman is better known, (better had he remain'd unknown) by an *ode to Benevolence*'. *Letters*, ed. Marrs, I, 151.

3 Thomas Davies (1712-1785) was an actor, author of a *Life of Garrick* and a bookseller. He is remembered now chiefly because it was at his shop that he introduced Boswell to Dr Johnson.

4 John Philip Kemble (1757-1823) made his London debut at the Old Drury Lane Theatre on 30 September, 1783 as Hamlet, thereafter one of his most popular roles.

5 Sarah Siddons (1755-1831) was the sister of John Philip Kemble and probably one of the greatest tragic actresses of all time. She retired from the stage in June, 1812, with a final performance of the Lady Macbeth that had been her most famous role.

6 Kemble and Siddons played the lead roles together in *Macbeth* at Drury Lane at various times between 1785 and 1794. There were sixteen performances at Drury Lane in 1794 and it was probably one or more of these that affected Lamb so profoundly, since it was late in 1794 that he wrote his sonnet about Mrs Siddons' Lady Macbeth (*Works*, V, 4).

7 *The Speaker*, published in 1774 by William Enfield, was an anthology of prose and verse extracts, designed as an aid to good elocution. It was popular as a school text-book and went into at least eleven editions by 1800.

8 *Clarissa, Or the History of a Young Lady*, a seven-volume novel by Samuel Richardson, published in 1748.

9 Bajazeth is Emperor of the Turks in Marlowe's *Tamburlaine* (c. 1587).

10 Posthumus is the husband of Imogen in *Cymbeline*.

11 Milton's *Paradise Lost*, Book VI, 338-340. The second word should read 'beseems'.

12 Thomas Betterton (c. 1635-1710) was the leading actor of the Restoration stage and greatly admired for his playing of Hamlet.

13 'with well-rounded utterance'; the phrase comes from Horace's *Ars Poetica*, 1. 323.

14 John Banks (c. 1650-1706) was author of eight tragedies; George Lillo (1693-1739) wrote the popular *London Merchant; or, the History of George Barnwell*, 1731, which Lamb mentions later.

15 It was the fashion to present *George Barnwell* for the apprentices at holiday times, particularly on Shrove Tuesday. Millwood is the adventurer who persuades George to rob his master and murder his uncle.

16 This reference has not been traced. It might possibly be a misquotation of 'Soule of the Age' from Jonson's 'To the memory of my beloved, the Author, Mr William Shakespeare', but if so it is wider of the mark than Lamb's misquotations usually are.

17 'like one of these harlotry players', *1 Henry IV*, II. iv. 385.

18 *The Gamester* (1753) by Edward Moore, is a domestic tragedy of the same kind as *George Barnwell* and Mrs Beverley is a character in it. Belvidera is in Thomas Otway's *Venice Preserved* (1682), Calista in Nicolas Rowe's *Fair Penitent* (1703), Isabella in Thomas Southerne's *The Fatal Marriage* (1694) and Euphrasia in Arthur Murphy's *The Grecian Daughter* (1772).

19 Aaron Hill (1695-1750), a playwright satirized by Pope in the *Dunciad*. Arthur Murphy (1727-1805), dramatist and adapter, wrote a *Life of David Garrick* (2 vols.), 1801. John Brown (1715-1766) was author of the plays *Barbarossa* and *Athelstane*.

20 From Shakespeare's Sonnet 111.

21 From Shakespeare's Sonnet 110.

22 From Shakespeare's Sonnet 29.

23 Nahum Tate (1652-1715) rewrote *King Lear* and Colley Cibber (1671-1757) adapted *Richard III*. See Lamb's letter to *The Spectator* on 'Shakespeare's Improvers', *Works* I, 321-323.

24 Milton's *Paradise Lost*, Book I, 1. 391.

25 The line in Cibber's *Richard III* reads 'If this have no Effect, she is immortal' (III. ii. 62).

26 George Frederick Cooke (1756-1811) made his debut as Richard III in 1800. For Lamb's detailed comments on Cooke's Richard, see Part I.

27 Glenalvon is a character in John Home's *Douglas* (1756).

28 John Philip Kemble first played Macbeth in London in 1785.

29   O heavens,
        If you do love old men, if your sweet sway
        Allow obedience, if you yourselves are old,
        Make it your cause. *King Lear*, II. iv. 188-191.

30 See note 43 below.

31 At the time this essay was written, gas-lighting had not yet been introduced to the theatres. The auditorium remained illuminated by candlelight throughout the performances.

32 Tom Brown (1663-1704) is perhaps best known as the author of the epigram 'I do not love thee, Dr Fell'. The line Lamb quotes is from Brown's 'Observations on Virgil, Ovid and Homer'.

33 Dryden collaborated with William Davenant on an adaptation entitled *The Tempest, or The Enchanted Island* (1667).

34 The Haymarket Theatre, where lectures on astronomy were often given.

35 Milton's Hymn 'On the Morning of Christ's Nativity', XIV. Lamb has substituted 'would' for 'will' in lines 1, 3, 4 and 5 of the quotation.

36 A costume-maker of Chancery Lane, London.

37 Mrs Siddons.

38 The three characters appear together in *The Merry Wives of Windsor*.

39 'Misery acquaints a man with strange bed-fellows', *The Tempest*, II. ii. 38.

40 Cordelia so describes Lear, IV. vii. 17.

41 Betty Careless (d. 1752) was a famous London courtesan.

42 *Rollo Duke of Normandy or The Bloody Brother* (c. 1619) is no longer ascribed to Francis Beaumont but to John Fletcher, possibly in collaboration with Massinger.

43 Lamb's quotation consists of passages from the last scene of *King Lear;* there are twelve further lines before the end of the play.

44   Let the great gods,
     That keep this dreadful pudder o'er our heads,
     Find out their enemies now. *King Lear*, III. ii. 49-51.

45 A reference to the Fool's song in *King Lear* which begins 'That sir which serves and seeks for gain/And follows but for form' (II. iv. 76-77).

46 Lamb's starting-point comes from Dryden's lines:
     Great wits are sure to madness near allied,
     And thin partitions do their bounds divide.
               Absalom and Achitophel, I, 11. 163-164.

47 From Abraham Cowley's ode 'On the Death of Mr William Hervey', Stanza 13.

48 'burning marl' is a quotation from *Paradise Lost*, Book I, 296 and 'Chaos and old Night' from Book I, 543.

49 Probably a misquotation of *King Lear*, IV. vii. 16: 'Th'untun'd and jarring senses'.

50 Proteus was a mythical sea deity who, because he could assume any shape he pleased, was used by Romantic writers as a symbol of the poetic imagination.

51 George Chapman's complete translation of the *Iliad* did not appear until 1611, though parts were published in 1598. The *Odyssey* was published in 1616.

Part III

1 Lamb saw the performance of *Twelfth Night* he here recalls when he was fifteen, or just turned sixteen. The cast he names performed on 3 November, 1790 and on 27 January, 16 February and 25 February, 1791. On all these occasions, however, Robert Palmer played Fabian. It is probable that Lamb made an error of transcription, because John Packer seems never to have played in *Twelfth Night* at all. See Charles Beecher Hogan, *Shakespeare in the Theatre, 1701-1800* (Oxford: Clarendon Press, 1957).

2 John Whitfield, John Hayman Packer, Robert Benson, John Burton, John Phillimore and William Blewitt Barrymore played bit parts at Drury Lane and Covent Garden in the last quarter of the eighteenth century.

3 Mistress of the Duke of Clarence, to whom she bore ten children, Dorothy Jordan (1761-1816) was thought to rival Sarah Siddons in some roles. She played Ophelia several times at Drury Lane in 1796 and 1797 but gave only one performance as Helena, on 12 December, 1794. She was popular in tomboy roles, especially as Hoyden in Vanbrugh's *The Relapse* and as Nell in Coffey's ballad opera *The Devil to Pay*. Lamb said of her elsewhere, 'she seemed one whom care could not come near; a privileged being sent to teach mankind what it most wants, joyousness.' ('Miss Kelly at Bath', *Four Dramatic Criticisms*, 1819)

4 The references to *Twelfth Night* are to II. iv. 108-117 and I. v. 254-255.

5 Jane Powell (d. 1831), formerly Mrs Farmer and later Mrs John James Renaud, played a number of Shakespearian heroines at Drury Lane, including Desdemona, Lady Macbeth and Portia.

6 Robert Bensley (1738-1817) made his debut as Pierre in Otway's *Venice Preserv'd* at Drury Lane on 2 October, 1765 and gave his final performance, playing opposite Mrs Siddons, on 6 May, 1796.

7 Hotspur's 'rant' is the speech in *1 Henry IV*, I. iii. 200-208. The 'Venetian incendiary' is Pierre in Otway's *Venice Preserv'd*.

8 Robert Baddeley (1736-1794) and William Parsons (1736-1795) played such Shakespearian roles as Flute, Pistol, Silence and Trinculo. They were better known for their original Moses and Crabtree respectively in Sheridan's *School for Scandal*. John Philip Kemble (1757-1823) was manager of the Drury Lane Theatre as well as its leading actor. Kemble played Malvolio on 19 March, 13 May and 31 May, 1789.

9 John Lambert (1619-1684) and Thomas, 3rd Baron Fairfax of Cameron (1612-1671) were leaders in Cromwell's army.

10 Olivia is more accurately 'the daughter of a count' (I. ii. 36).

11 The quotations from *Twelfth Night* in this paragraph are from III. iv. 60, I. v. 85 and V. i. 366.

12 Cervantes' Don Quixote. In his essay 'On the Productions of Modern Art', Lamb complains that artists depict Quixote 'in the shallow hope of exciting mirth' when the 'pitiable infirmity' (the same phrase is used of Malvolio) leads him '*always from within*, into half-ludicrous, but more than half-compassionable and admirable errors.' *Works*, II. 233.

13 In Greek mythology, Hyperion is father of the sun and moon but is often used as a synonym for the sun.

14 Marlowe's *Edward II*, V. i. 66.

15 *Twelfth Night*, V. i. 362.

16 James William Dodd (1734-1796) was the original Sir Benjamin Backbite in *The School for Scandal*, and was best as a fop. Lamb mentions below (see note 20) Dodd's other famous roles.

17 William Lovegrove (1778-1816) made a name in comic parts at Drury Lane.

18 Stark naked.

19 Lamb was born in the Inner Temple, one of the four buildings in London in which the societies of English barristers are housed. Lamb's father was clerk to one of the senior barristers. See Lamb's essay on 'The Old Benchers of the Inner Temple.' Sir Francis Bacon (1561-1626) was a member of Gray's Inn, called to the bar in 1582.

20 Foppington is a character in Vanbrugh's *The Relapse*, Tattle is in Congreve's *Love for Love*, Backbite in Sheridan's *School for Scandal*, Acres in Sheridan's *The Rivals* and Fribble in Garrick's *Miss in her Teens*.

21 And they who to be sure of Paradise
Dying put on the weeds of Dominic.
Paradise Lost, Book III, 478-479.
St Dominic, founder of the Dominican Order, practised asceticism and poverty.

22 Richard Suett (1755-1805) made his first appearance at Drury Lane in 1780, where he was considered a fine comedian, especially playing Shakespeare's fools.

23 Suett was buried in St Paul's Churchyard, but Lucas asserts that he had been a chorister at Westminster Abbey. See *Works*, II, p. 394.

24 Falstaff in *2 Henry IV*, I. ii. 179.

25 'And looks commercing with the skies', Milton, 'Il Penseroso', 1. 39.

26 For William Parsons, see note 8 above.

27 Charles Mathews (1776-1835) was best known for his mimicry. He developed a form of one-man show in which he played a wide variety of characters.

28 John Dryden's 'Epigram on Milton', 1. 5.

29 Robin Goodfellow is Puck in *A Midsummer Night's Dream*. The words are from his song at the beginning of Act II.

30 John Bannister (1760-1836) was the original Don Ferolo Whiskerandos in Sheridan's *The Critic* and played many comic roles at Drury Lane.

31 Thomas Morton's *Children in the Wood* (1793) was one of Lamb's favourite children's plays. In 'Old China', he recalls sitting in the one-shilling gallery to see 'Bannister and Mrs Bland in the Children in the Wood.'

32 'Love is too young to know what conscience is', Sonnet 151.

33 Since Vesta was the patroness of the Vestal Virgins, 'Vesta's days' are presumably days of innocence.

34 Robert Palmer (1754-1817), who played important roles at both Covent Garden and Drury Lane, was brother of John (1744-1798) 'the elder Palmer' mentioned below. John played Falstaff as well as Sir Toby and he created the part of Joseph Surface in *The School for Scandal*.

35 John Moody (1728-1813) was an Irish actor who played the original Lord Burghley in *The Critic*. He had notoriously sluggish and immobile features.

36 Captain Absolute is a character in Sheridan's *The Rivals*; Dick Amlet is in Vanbrugh's *The Conspiracy*.

37 Young Wilding is a character in Samuel Foote's *The Liar*; Joseph Surface is in Sheridan's *School for Scandal*.

38 Congreve's *Love for Love*, IV. vi.

39 *The Tempest*, I. ii. 266-267.

40 Addison's *Spectator*, I, 1 March, 1711.

41 John Ogilby (1600-1676), Scottish topographer, printer and mapmaker, became an important London publisher after the Restoration, when he produced his atlases of Africa, America and Asia.

42 Leo Africanus was a Cordovan Moor whose account of his travels in northern Africa (*Africae Descriptio*, 1526) was for a long time the chief source of information about the Sudan. Of the remaining authorities listed, only Louis del Marmol's *Descripcion General de Africa* (1571) was published before Shakespeare wrote *The Tempest*.

43 The narrator of this essay purports to be a man who, having been wrongly convicted of crime, hung from the noose for four minutes before a reprieve came.

44 See *Hamlet*, V. i. 41-49.

45 *Measure for Measure*, IV. iii. 19-43.

Part IV

1 *Letters*, ed. Lucas. III, 82.

2 Although Marlowe's name is on the earliest title-page, this play is now attributed to Thomas Dekker. See *The Dramatic Works of Thomas Dekker*, ed. Fredson Bowers (Cambridge University Press, 1961) IV.

3 The phrase 'in King Cambyses' vein' is Falstaff's reference (*1 Henry IV*, II. iv. 376) to the bombastic hero of Thomas Preston's tragicomedy *Cambyses, King of Persia*.

4 'To th'huffing braggart, puft Nobility', John Donne, 'Satire IV', l. 164.

5 Pistol is Shakespeare's comic braggart. He appears in *2 Henry IV*, *Henry V* and *The Merry Wives of Windsor*.

6 Marlowe's lines:
> Holla, ye pamper'd jades of Asia!
> What, can ye draw but twenty miles a day?
> > (*2 Tamburlaine*, IV. iii. 1-2)

are violated by Pistol in *2 Henry IV*, II. iv. 154-157:
> Shall pack-horses,
> And hollow pamper'd jades of Asia,
> Which cannot go but thirty mile a day,
> Compare with Caesars. . . .

7 An additional passage in the 1808 volume reads at this point: 'Shylock, in the midst of his savage purpose, is a man. His motives, feelings, resentments, have something human in them. "If you wrong us, shall we not revenge?"'

8 In the volume of 1808, the note reads, 'It is indeed an agony and bloody sweat.'

9 Robert Lovelace is the 'villain' of Samuel Richardson's novel *Clarissa* (see Part II, note 8). Sir Charles Sedley (1639-1701), George Villiers, 2nd Duke of Buckingham (1627-1687) and John Wilmot, Earl of Rochester (1647-1680) were notorious debauchees.

10 One of the witty young lovers in *Love's Labour's Lost*.

11 The quotations are from Milton's 'The Passion', VIII:
> And I (for grief is easily beguild)
> Might think th'infection of my sorrows loud,
> Had got a race of mourners on som pregnant cloud.

12 From Milton's Preface to *Samson Agonistes*.

13 *Paradise Lost*, IV, 1-2.

14 The description of a desirable dress for a merchant is as follows:
> In a black bever belt, ash colour plain,
> A Florentine cloth-o'silver jerkin, sleeves
> White satin cut on tinsel, then long stock;
> French panes embroider'd, goldsmith's work:.

15 Sir Thomas Gresham (1519-1579), English financier and founder of the Royal Exchange. The quotation following the mention of the 'Change' has not been traced.

16 *Othello*, V. i. 356.

17 John Reynolds was the early seventeenth century author of *The Triumphs of God's Revenge Against Murder*.

18 A line omitted here from the original reads: 'This scene has much of Shakespeare's manner in the sweetness and goodnaturedness of it'.

19 *Hamlet*, III. iv. The quoted words in the following sentence echo *Hamlet* II .ii. 584-588 and 557.

20 'On horror's head horrors accumulate'; *Othello*, III, iii. 374. 'Terrify babes, my Lord, with painted devils', *The White Devil* III, ii. 147.

21 Skelton's translation of *Don Quixote*, Book II, ch. 6.

22 Shakespeare's sonnet 95.

23 The two dirges are as follows:
> Call for the robin-red-breast and the wren,
> Since o'er shady groves they hover,
> And with leaves and flow'rs do cover
> The friendless bodies of unburied men.
> Call unto his funeral dole
> The ant, the field-mouse, and the mole
> To rear him hillocks, that shall keep him warm,
> And (when gay tombs are robb'd) sustain no harm, —
> But keep the wolf far thence, that's foe to men,
> For with his nails he'll dig them up agen.
>> (*The White Devil*, V. iv. 95-104).

> Full fathom five thy father lies;
> Of his bones are coral made;
> Those are pearls that were his eyes;
> Nothing of him that doth fade
> But doth suffer a sea-change
> Into something rich and strange.
> Sea-nymphs hourly ring his knell:
> > Ding-dong
> Hark! now I hear them — Ding-dong bell.
>
> (*The Tempest*, I. ii. 375-404).

24 Milton, *Samson Agonistes*, 1016-1017.

25 Sir Philip Sidney's *Arcadia* (published 1590) is a pastoral romance incorporating many of the stock elements to be found in the love themes of Shakespearian comedy.

26 John Donne, 'Elegie XVI: On his Mistris'.

27 *Comus* is Milton's masque glorifying the virtue of chastity; Hermia and Lysander are two of the young lovers in *A Midsummer Night's Dream*. For *Arcadia*, see Note 25 above.

28 The goddess Diana was the patroness of virginity.

29 Bishop Jeremy Taylor (1613-1667), author of *The Rule and Exercises of Holy Living* (1650) and *The Rule and Exercises of Holy Dying* (1651), was much read and admired by Lamb.

30 John Bull is a nickname for the typical Englishman.

31 See Part II, note 7.

32 ' "Aroint thee, witch!" the rump-fed ronyon cries.' *Macbeth*, I. iii. 6. 'the crow/Makes wing to th'rooky wood;' *Macbeth*, III. ii. 50-51.

Bibliography

Barnet, Sylvan. "Charles Lamb and the Tragic Malvolio." *Philological Quarterly*, 33 (April, 1954), 178-188.

Barnett, George L. *Charles Lamb. The Evolution of Elia.* New York: Haskell House, 1973.

Boas, F. S. "Charles Lamb and the Elizabethan Dramatists." *Essays and Studies*, 29 (1944), 62-81.

Bradley, A. C. *Oxford Lectures on Poetry.* London: Macmillan, 1909.

Coldwell, Joan. "The Playgoer as Critic: Charles Lamb on Shakespeare's Characters." *Shakespeare Quarterly*, 26 (Spring, 1975), 184-195.

Coleridge, S. T. *Coleridge's Miscellaneous Criticism*, ed. T. M. Raysor. London: Constable, Co., 1936.

——————. *Coleridge's Shakespearean Criticism*, ed. T. M. Raysor, London: Constable and Co., 1930.

Cornwall, Barry. *Charles Lamb.* Boston: Roberts Brothers, 1866.

Hayden, John O. *The Romantic Reviewers, 1802-1824.* Chicago: University of Chicago Press, 1968.

Hazlitt, William. "Characters of Shakespear's Plays," *Complete Works*, ed. P. P. Howe. vol. III. London: J. M. Dent, 1930.

Hunt, Leigh. *Critical Essays on the Performers of the London Theatres.* London: John Hunt, 1807.

Lamb, Charles and Mary. *Letters*, ed. Edwin W. Marrs, Jr. Ithaca, N.Y.: Cornell University Press, 1975-1976.

——————. *Letters*, ed. E. V. Lucas. London: J. M. Dent and Methuen, 1935.

——————. *Works*, ed. E. V. Lucas. London: Methuen, 1903-1905.

Lucas, E. V. *The Life of Charles Lamb.* London: Methuen, 1905.

Pater, Walter. *Appreciations.* London: Macmillan, 1889.

Randel, Fred V. *The World of Elia.* Port Washington, N.Y.: Kennikat Press, 1975.

Robinson, Henry Crabb. *Diary, Reminiscences and Correspondence,* ed. Thomas Sadler. London, 1869.

Roe, Frederick W. "Charles Lamb and Shakespeare." *Shakespeare Studies* (University of Wisconsin, 1916), 276-300.

Russell, W. Clark. *Representative Actors.* London: F. Warne, n.d.

Swinburne, A. C. *The Age of Shakespeare.* London: Chatto and Windus, 1908.

Thompson, A. H. "The Nineteenth Century," *Cambridge History of English Literature,* vol. XII. Cambridge: Cambridge University Press, 1961.

Tillyard, E. M. W. *Lamb's Criticism.* Cambridge: Cambridge University Press, 1923.

Watson, George. *The Literary Critics.* Harmondsworth, Middlesex: Penguin Books, 1962.

Wellek, René. *A History of Modern Criticism, 1750-1950.* New Haven: Yale University Press, 1955.

Index

Lamb, Charles: attitude of
contemporaries to, 11, 66; attitude
of later critics to, 15; birthplace
of, 167n19; his collaboration on
Falstaff Letters, 12; his
conversation, 11; his imaginative
response to Shakespeare, 12; on
dreams, 23; and the *London
Magazine*, 27; his reading, 12,
161n6; and *The Reflector*, 27, 52;
his share of *Tales from Shakespear*,
14-15, 81; his study of
Shakespeare's contemporaries, 14,
66; his theatre-going, 12-13, 17;
his view of Shakespeare's
characters, 13-14, 48-49
Lamb, Mary, 81
Lillo, George, 30, 163n14. See also
London Merchant
London Magazine, 23, 24, 50, 64
*London Merchant; or the History
of George Barnwell* (by George
Lillo), 31, 35-36; 163n14 and n15
Love for Love (by William
Congreve), 61, 167n20, 168n38
Lovegrove, William, 56, 166n17

Marlowe, Christopher, 67, 168n2
Marlowe, Christopher, works by:
Doctor Faustus, 68, *Edward II*, 14
67, 166n14, *The Jew of Malta*,
67-68, *Tamburlaine*, 67, 163n9,
168n6
Marston, John, works by: *Antonio
and Mellida*, 69-70, *What You
Will*, 70
Massinger, Philip, 67, 165n42. See
also *The Virgin Martyr*
Mathews, Charles, 59, 167n27
Merry Devil of Edmonton, 70-71
Middleton, Thomas, 71-72. See also
The Witch
Milton, John, 12, 36, 68, 70, 75
Milton, John, works by: *Comus*, 78,
"Il Penseroso", 167n25, "On the
Morning of Christ's Nativity",
164n35, *Paradise Lost*, 25, 163n11,
164n24, 165n48, 167n21, 169n13,
"The Passion", 169n11, *Samson*

Agonistes, 169n12, 170n24
Moody, John, 60, 167n35
Murphy, Arthur, 33, 164n19

Packer, John Hayman, 50, 165n1 and
n2
Palmer, John, 60, 167n34
Palmer, Robert, 60, 165n1, 167n34
Parsons, William, 53, 59, 166n8,
167n26
Phillimore, John, 51, 165n2
Powel, Jane, 51, 166n5

Quin, James, 18, 162n3

Rake's Progress (by William
Hogarth), 42-45
Reflector, The, 24, 50, 65
Rowe, Nicholas, 163n18
Rowley, William, 72

Shakespeare, William: as actor, 34;
and his audience, 65; and his
characters, 13, 25, 29, 31, 35-36,
37-39, 45, 48, 49, 69; and his
depiction of women, 74; and his
imagination, 13, 32, 75; and his
language, 22, 71, 77-78, 80; and his
sanity, 47; his plays: adaptations
of, 13, 17, 19, 30; extracting from,
79; their mixture of tragedy and
comedy, 45; their naturalness, 31;
in relation to contemporary plays,
14, 66-78; Romantic attitudes to,
11-12; their uniqueness, 33; their
unsuitability for the stage, 28
Shakespeare, William, works by:
All's Well that Ends Well, 49, 51,
76; *As You Like It*: Jaques in, 79;
Cymbeline, 163n10; Imogen in, 29,
33, 163n10; Posthumus in, 28, 29,
163n10; *Hamlet*, 27, 45, 49, 65, 81,
133-147; Gertrude in, 41; Gravedigger in, 45, 65; Hamlet in, 18,
25, 27, 29-30, 32, 33, 41, 48, 73;
King in, 48, 49; Ophelia in, 32, 33,
51 (Mrs Jordan as); Polonius in,
32; *Henry IV*, 163n17, 166n7;
Falstaff in, 58, 167n24, 168n3;

82 83
84 85 86

88
89
91
92
93

822-33 Lamb, Charles
D
LAM   Charles Lamb on
          Shakespeare
                    820788

DATE			
DEC 8 '82			
MAR 1 6 '83			
JAN 6			
APR 1 1987			
FEB 5 '88			
3-16-8?			
DE 0 2 '97			